Editor:
Charles Payne, M.A., M.F.A.

Editor in Chief:
Sharon Coan, M.S. Ed.

Creative Director:
Elayne Roberts

Art Coordination Assistant:
Cheri Macoubrie Wilson

Cover Artist:
Tina DeLeon Macabitas

Product Manager:
Phil Garcia

Imaging:
Charles Payne, M.A., M.F.A.

Acknowledgements:
HyperStudio® is a registered trademark of Roger Wagner Publishing, Inc.
Apple, the Apple Logo, Macintosh, *AppleWorks,* and *ClarisWorks* are registered trademarks of Apple Computer, Inc.
The Writing Center™ is a registered trademark of The Learning Company.

Publishers:
Rachelle Cracchiolo, M.S. Ed.
Mary Dupuy Smith, M.S. Ed.

INTEGRATING TECHNOLOGY into the Science Curriculum

INTERMEDIATE

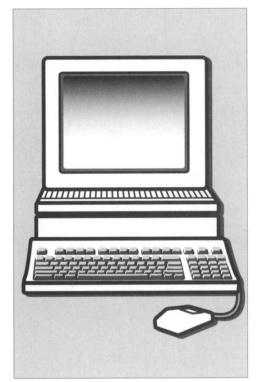

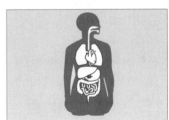

Author:

Paula G. Patton

Teacher Created Materials, Inc.
6421 Industry Way
Westminster, CA 92683
www.teachercreated.com

ISBN-1-55734-428-8

©1999 Teacher Created Materials, Inc.
Revised, 1999

Made in U.S.A.

TABLE OF CONTENTS

TABLE OF CONTENTS (cont.)

WELCOME

Education should be about learning—meaningful learning—rather than memorizing and parroting one teacher's or one textbook's insights. Education is an adventure, and in exploring interesting issues and questions, we must use all the tools at our disposal. Student investigation and discovery, while always a goal, can be more attainable with technology, and our curriculum must reflect this. The curriculum should prepare children for the challenges of the 21st century and the Age of Information. Every classroom can have up-to-date encyclopedias, access to huge libraries, and personal contact with experts in nearly every field. Each class can have the tools of a publishing company to show the results of the students' work utilizing many different media.

However, all the technology in the world is not going to aid learning if the teacher is not comfortable with it. That is the purpose of this book: to provide teachers with some suggestions, ideas, and "jumping-off" places to start their own meaningful relationship with technology in the curriculum.

This book is one in a series of 12 on integrating technology into the curriculum. There are four subject areas—math, science, language arts, and social studies—on each of three levels—primary, intermediate, and challenging. Each book contains management ideas to help you set up your computer lab and use the computer to organize your records. Also included are lesson plans and activities for using technology in your curriculum so that you have technology—it doesn't have you.

HARDWARE

Hardware is the term used when referring to the actual electronic machinery used for technology. When using technology in the classroom, there are many different types of hardware tools and tool combinations available to you and your students. The following list offers brief descriptions of popular hardware devices.

Computer

A computer is an electronic machine which processes data. Computers take information (data) that you put in (input) and then do something with the information (output). The output is given in a way that is understandable, such as text or pictures seen on the computer monitor or information on paper printed by the printer. A computer basically does three things: accepts data, processes data, outputs information. Virtually every computer on the market today is now a multimedia computer. A multimedia computer contains the monitor, CD-ROM drive, modem, sound card, and microphone all built into one unit. The keyboard is attached by a cord.

Monitor: This is another word for the computer screen.

Keyboard: A keypad with alpha, numeric, and function keys is used to communicate with the computer.

Mouse: This small handheld device connected to the keyboard allows you to control the position of the cursor on the screen. Move the mouse on a flat surface such as a static-free mouse pad or the top of your desk.

CD-ROM: CD-ROM stands for compact disk, read only memory. The CD-ROM player will read the contents of the CD-ROM and present the images onto the computer monitor.

Microphone: This device allows you to record sounds. A microphone can be built into the computer or can be an external device which connects via cable.

Modem: A modem is a device that allows a computer to communicate to other computers via the telephone line. The speed of the modem is called the baud rate. The faster the baud rate, the faster you can access the Internet and download files.

Printer: A separate piece of hardware, the printer connects to the computer via cable. The printer prints text and images onto paper. Common types of printers are laser printers, ink-jet printers, dot-matrix printers, and imagesetters.

HARDWARE *(cont.)*

Laserdisc Player

Also known as a videodisc player, this piece of hardware is used to play laserdiscs. A laserdisc looks like a CD-ROM disc except it is larger, about the size of a standard long-playing phonograph record (remember those?), and contains permanently stored large quantities of information in the format of text, graphics, movies, and sound. The laserdisc player is about the size of a VCR and similar in its features. You control the laserdisc manually by choosing the appropriate buttons or with a remote control or bar code reader.

Scanner

A scanner allows you to copy an image which is outside of the computer and then import the image back into the computer. There are two types of scanners, flatbed and handheld. A flatbed scanner works very much like a copy machine where items to be copied are placed flat onto the glass. Handheld scanners are small enough to fit into your hand and roll over the flat image while taking a "picture" of the image. Images are then saved to a floppy disk or directly onto the computer hard drive.

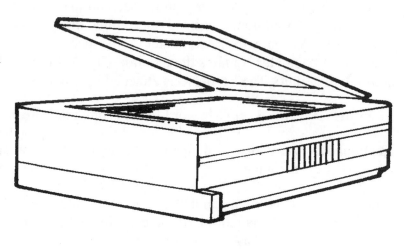

Digital Camera

This handy device allows you to take pictures of people, places, and events away from the computer and then later use these images for multimedia projects. A digital camera looks and operates very much like a 35–mm camera. The primary difference is the digital camera outputs images in digital form instead of on photographic film. These digital images can be stored either to floppy disk or directly onto the hard drive of the computer.

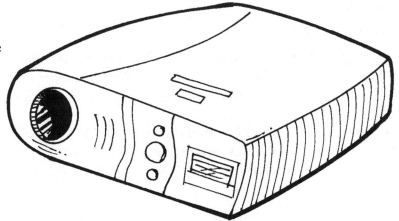

Note:

- Both scanners and digital cameras are useful pieces of hardware with unique advantages. A scanner is best used when copying one-dimensional images (e.g., student illustrations, writing samples, maps) where a digital camera is best used to capture three-dimensional images (e.g., students engaged in activities, field trips, artwork such as sculpture, science experiments).

HARDWARE *(cont.)*

Video Camera

At one time, video cameras were quite large, heavy, and could only be held on your shoulder while recording. Now video cameras are small enough to fit into the palm of your hand. The video camera (or "camcorder," as it is often called) records events and activities as they occur into a movie format and saves the images to tape. With the appropriate software and cables, you can connect the video camera to your multimedia computer, download these movies, and then save them as files directly onto the computer hard drive.

Tripod

A three-legged device that holds the video camera in place, the legs of the tripod can be adjusted to different heights. Tripods are used for long-term and remote-control recording.

TV as a Presentation Tool

Use a television as a presentation tool by connecting your computer to the TV. This is an easy and cost-effective strategy to obtain large-screen projection for the classroom. There are several systems available which will allow you to connect the computer to the television. Some popular systems include L-TV Portable and L-TV Internal Card (Focus Enhancements), TelevEyes/Plus and TelevEyes/Pro (Digital Vision) and The Presenter Mac/PC 3 (Consumer Technology). For older computer models, sometimes all that is necessary is an RF modulator or Y-splitter cable (both found at electronics stores).

SOFTWARE

General Software Suggestions

Title: *ClarisWorks*

Publisher: Claris Corporation

This is an integrated software package that combines word processing, painting, drawing, spreadsheet, database, and communication capabilities.

Title: *HyperStudio*

Publisher: Roger Wagner Publishing

This multimedia authoring software offers the ability to bring together text, sound, graphics, and video. *HyperStudio* allows for accessing data on the Internet, creating and editing QuickTime movies, built-in image capture, Mac-Windows project compatibility, and a wide range of file-type compatibility for graphics and sound.

Title: *Imagination Express*

Publisher: Edmark

Students easily create interactive electronic books and printed stories. Each destination contains a variety of backgrounds and hundreds of stickers. The students simply drag the stickers onto the backgrounds and then add text, narration, music or sound effects. These programs also include a movie-making feature that allows students to drag stamps across the screen, then replay their motion. Students can also browse through fact books that give information about each destination. Separate destinations include: Castle, Neighborhood, Rain Forest, Ocean, Pyramids, and Time Trip, U.S.A.

Title: *Kid Pix Studio*

Publisher: Brøderbund

This multimedia paint and animation program includes six projects: Kid Pix, Moopies, SlideShow, Wacky TV, Stampimator, and Digital Puppets. Students can use SlideShow to create their own animated stories, photo essays, and presentations. Features include over 1,300 animated and rubber stamps, 50 Wacky Brushes and dozens of multicolor fill patterns, text tools, song clips, and sound effects.

Title: *The Print Shop*

Publisher: Brøderbund

Users can create and print six different types of projects, including greeting cards, signs, banners, calendars, letterhead, and labels. Students can choose from over 1,000 graphics to create full-page designs and layouts.

SOFTWARE *(cont.)*

Title: *The Writing Center*

Publisher: The Learning Company

This simple word-processing program provides students with templates to create stories, newsletters, menus, letters, flyers, and other text-based projects.

INTERNET IN THE INTERMEDIATE CLASSROOM

Internet:

The Internet is the most widespread computer network. It provides many services that are useful as educational tools.

World Wide Web:

The World Wide Web (WWW) is one of the most exciting Internet services to be used for education. To access the WWW you need a WWW browser (*Netscape Navigator, Microsoft Internet Explorer,* etc.). These browsers interpret and display documents found on the WWW. Links within WWW documents can take you quickly to other related documents.

While the Internet provides a multitude of learning opportunities, some precautions must be taken before sending your students to the World Wide Web. Before using any activities, it is strongly recommended you verify the suggested Web sites and make sure that information is appropriate for educational activities. Don't forget to preview links on the sites with caution and keep a keen eye out for unsuitable material. Further, Web sites (and their links) frequently change addresses or become unavailable for myriad reasons.

Teacher Created Materials attempts to offset this ongoing problem by posting changes of URL's on our Web site. Check our home page at **www.teachercreated.com** for updates on this book.

Search Engines:

Search engines are helpful for researching just about any topic. The following URL addresses assist users in locating information:

Alta Vista	*http://www.altavista.com*
Excite	*http://www.excite.com*
InfoSeek	*http://www2.Infoseek.com*
Lycos	*http://www.lycos.com*
WebCrawler	*http://www.webcrawler.com*
Yahoo!	*http://www.yahoo.com*
Hotbot	*http://www.hotbot.com*
LookSmart	*http://www.looksmart.com*

Newsgroups:

Newsgroups are discussion groups on all kinds of subjects. The messages are posted to the group, and anyone can answer.

INTERNET IN THE INTERMEDIATE CLASSROOM *(cont.)*

Internet Relay Chat (IRC):

This is an interactive communication system where users can chat with people from all over the world. Everything is typed instead of spoken. IRC is made up of topic-specific channels. When you connect to IRC, you will see a listing of the current active channels and the topics being discussed. Teachers should use caution when letting students explore these channels.

- A variety of K–12 newsgroup and IRC projects and activities can be found at the below address. *http://www.useekufind.com/*

E-mail:

Electronic mail is one of the most widely used services on the Internet. It is fast, convenient, and easy to use. Students can quickly send messages all around the world. Messages arrive within minutes of being sent. *Eudora* is a widely used e-mail program. *Eudora* allows users to send, retrieve, file, re-send, save, and edit mail. It handles text, binary, video, and audio mail, and it runs on multiple platforms.

Mailing Lists/List servers:

Mailing lists is a way for a group of people with common interests to share information. List server software has been developed to automate the administration of mailing lists. Requests for information or to subscribe (participate) or unsubscribe (drop out) are automatically handled by a central host. Teachers can subscribe to hundreds of mailing lists. One of those mailing lists is HILITES (HILITES@gsn.org). All messages sent to the HILITES list must meet certain criteria before they are posted. This is to ensure that subscribers to HILITES mailboxes won't be flooded with inappropriate or off-subject messages. HILITES is reserved for K–12 teachers to announce learning projects that will engage students in other classes in one or more collaborative learning activities.

Collaborative Telecommunications Project Postings:

The Internet offers an effective way to teach students to both communicate and collaborate by connecting teams of students with classrooms around the world. Thousands of educational collaborative projects exist. The Global School Net (GSN) Internet Project Registry (http://www.gsh.org/gsn/proj/index.html) is designed for busy teachers searching for appropriate online projects to integrate into their classrooms. This registry is the one central place where teachers can find projects from the GSN and other organizations such as I*EARN, IECC, NASA, GLOBE, Academy One, TIES, Tenet, and TERC. Projects are listed by the month in which they begin.

MANAGEMENT

Cooperative Learning

Work on the computer lends itself well to cooperative learning. Teams of three to five students working at a single computer tend to produce more creative output than one single student. One idea generates another, and the whole team profits. Each group should, ideally, have mixed abilities and interests. Even in a one-computer classroom, cooperative learning works. You can have groups involved in different aspects of the project, some at the computer while others are involved in essential, but non-computer, modules.

Configurations

My favorite computer lab configuration has learning centers. A 15-computer lab, for example, would have a group of five computers loaded with instructional software. The students could play math games, do language arts tutorials, or learn a foreign language. There are many wonderful instructional programs available. Just pick up an educational software catalog, and you can see the wide array of choices available to you. Five is also the usual number of licenses in a "lab pack," so your software purchases would be simpler. These programs usually require little monitoring, so the teacher's time is less fragmented. This is the "Games Center."

The next center would have five computers loaded with electronic encyclopedias, informational disks—*Library of the Future, Animals, Dinosaurs, Atlas of U.S. History,* etc.—and Internet access. This is the Research Center. Your scanner and cable for the digital camera would also go here.

Five computers with word processors and desktop publishing programs would make up the "Publishing Center."

A large table with chairs in the center of the room would be the "Writing Center." This would be used for projects in the planning stage, proofreading, and anything needing paper and pencil work.

The "Idea" table would have prompts for writing, inspirational material, simple science experiments, teacher and student created displays of interest—anything that will spark ideas, curiosity, interest.

So here we have a lab for 25 students or more with only 15 computers and as few as two printers.

Another important part of a computer lab is the "Information Center" for teachers. A table near the door with a small bulletin board behind it will hold the things that teachers bringing their students to the lab will need.

- Lab Schedule
- Software Manuals

MANAGEMENT *(cont.)*

- Software Help—This is a binder with space for teachers to jot down helpful hints that they have discovered about certain programs. Also frequently asked questions may be answered here by the lab manager. Handouts from technology staff development or workshops can also go in this binder. Teachers who are feeling "dumb" because they can't remember what we learned in that workshop on word processing last week can look here and save face.

- Notes to the Lab Manager—Maybe a program your students used today has a glitch. Perhaps the J key on computer #3 is loose. The mouse on computer #7 will only move the pointer left to right, not up and down. Mrs. Jones absolutely has to have *Godzilla Learns to Type*. Write it on the clipboard, and the lab manager will have a record of it.

- Brag Book—"My students made a *Power Point* presentation called 'A Tour of the School.'" "You ought to see the Mother's Day card little Johnny designed." "The reports on wildflowers that the fifth graders did were awesome." Put examples of successful projects in a binder for other teachers to see, along with explanations of how they were done. Cooperative learning is not just for kids.

- On the bulletin board can be posted projects in progress, upcoming workshops, and new software, whatever is of technological interest to teachers.

More Management Tips

- Teach in small bites. After about five minutes of sitting and listening to someone tell them how to do something on the computer, children (and adults) start to lose concentration. They need to be instructed on one or two things and then allowed to see how those one or two things work. Start every activity with a "tech talk," a short period of instruction, and then some time on the computer. Even if the children are familiar with the program, there are always tricks and short-cuts to be shared.

- Help with your hands in your pockets. It is very difficult not to just do it for them when a student is having trouble. However, if you do, then they still will not have the skill. Explain how to do the task. Let the student do it himself. He will have the pride of accomplishment and will not have the damage to his self-esteem that comes from someone, even a peer, taking the mouse away and saying, "Here, let me do that."

- Have a disk for each child. If the work is saved on a floppy disk, then when there is time, the project can be continued on the classroom computer, if you have one. This also prevents another student from another class from possibly altering or erasing work saved on the lab computers.

- Invest in some plastic hanging shoe bags, the kind that hang on the closet door and have multiple slots for putting shoes in. These are ideal for keeping up with your students' disks. When you enter the lab, hang up the shoe bags. Each child can get her own disk and start to work. At the end of the session, the students put their disks back in the slots, the teacher removes the holder from the hooks and folds it up to take it back to the classroom.

MANAGEMENT *(cont.)*

Evaluation and Assessment

There are many types of assessment that work well with technology. A rubric can be used. Checklists work fine. I have gained significant insight by having students write paragraphs about "How Well I Did on My Project." These types of assessments require the students to think about the projects and things learned. They also cause the students to be aware of areas that need work. When the students think out these things for themselves, they have more meaning than if I put a lot of red Xs on a paper test and hand it back to be crammed in a locker or backpack and never seen again. The checklists, paragraphs, or rubrics can be kept and consulted by the students when planning the next project.

Checklist for *Power Point* Presentation

Is the planning sheet complete?	
What kind of software did I use?	
What kind of hardware did I use?	
Did I have any problems with hardware or software? What kinds?	
How did I solve these problems?	
Did I do my research?	
What could I have done to improve the content?	
What was the part of the project that I was most pleased with? Why?	
What new skills did I acquire?	
What other new things did I learn?	
How would I change the project if I did it again?	

MANAGEMENT *(cont.)*

State Report

State Report Collaborative Project Rubric			
5 points	**10 points**	**15 points**	**20 points**
Required Elements*	The stack includes fewer than 5 of the required elements.	The stack includes 5–7 of the required elements.	The stack includes at least 8 of the required elements.	The stack includes all 10 of the required elements.
Internet Connection	The student does not use the Internet to gather resources.	The student browses the Internet, but is unable to find resources to use.	The student utilizes the Internet to get information or pictures for stack.	The student creates a link from the stack to an appropriate Internet site.
Navigation/ Organization	Information is not organized well; navigation is difficult.	Information is organized and linked for linear navigation.	A table of contents card organizes and links the info for nonlinear navigation.	Buttons are cleverly used to link information in a creative way.
Mechanics	Spelling and punctuation errors are distracting.	Spelling and punctuation errors are evident.	Errors in spelling and punctuation are minor and few.	There are no errors in spelling or punctuation.
Overall Impression	Cards are not neatly done and include too much or too little information.	Cards could be neater and contain too much or too little information.	Cards are colorful and attractive and include appropriate amounts of information.	Cards are very attractive and relate information in a creative way.
Collaboration	The MS student does not get input from the 4th grade student.	The MS student sometimes includes the 4th grader in decisions.	The MS student includes the 4th grader when making decisions about the stack.	The MS student clearly explains each step; the 4th grader is actively involved.

*Required elements = location, capital, fame (for people or historical landmarks), waterways, population, resources, industries, climate, landforms, state symbols.

Thanks to Tammy Worcester for this rubric.

ELECTRONIC PORTFOLIOS

Create electronic portfolios for your students. They take up very little space and are easily updated, easily accessed, and easily located. ("Now, under which stack of papers is Johnny's math paper that I wanted you to see?")

- You can have pictures, work samples, sounds, drawings, and even movies in each child's portfolio.

- The students can create and edit parts of their own portfolios, gaining computer skills and pride of accomplishment, and it gets done in less time!

- What a wonderful open house activity! Each child can get his disk, show his expertise in loading the program, and then have the portfolio there for viewing.

Materials: scanner, digital camera, and multimedia software program such as *Power Point, HyperStudio*

Procedure: Create an electronic portfolio for each child. Some things that might be included in this portfolio are

- samples of writing. These can be typed in directly, imported, or scanned if you want to also show handwriting.

- samples of reading. These can be recorded directly into *HyperStudio* or *Power Point*.

- samples of artwork. Scan these or use a drawing program, or both.

- journals.

- computer projects.

- athletic accomplishments. Use a digital camera or scan a photograph.

- U.I.L. competition.

- anything that is important to the students, their parents, future teachers, the world.

Before the Computer:

- Plan on paper what to put on each card of your stack.

On the Computer:

- Create the cards of your stack, including general information about your school, your class, the year, etc.

- Add text boxes and buttons.

- Save your stack as "template."

- Open the template and have the students modify the template to fit their needs.

- Be sure to "Save As" and change the name to that of the student.

DATABASE OF STUDENTS

By keeping a database of your students, you can save yourself lots of time and be creatively personal with your students.

Materials: a database program such as the ones in *Microsoft Works*, *ClarisWorks* and *Microsoft Office*; a list of your students' information

On the Computer:

- Create a database with the following fields:

  First Name

  Last Name

  Parent/Guardian Name

  Address

  City

  State

  Zip Code

  Birthday

  Phone Number

- Enter information about each student.

Possible Uses:

- Merge the database into a general welcoming letter to the parents at the beginning of the year and when you need to communicate throughout the year. The parents will appreciate seeing, "Dear Mr. and Mrs. Jones, I am happy to have Katrina in my class this year. Here are some things she will need...." instead of "Dear Parent, I am happy to have your son/daughter/ward in my class this year. Here are some things he/she will need...."

- Using the label portion of your word processor, create nametags for your students at the beginning of the year. Enter "Hello, I'm" and then merge with the database.

- Again using the label portion of your word processor, design stand-up place cards for each student's desk. These are handy at the beginning of the year and at open house.

- Make personalized bookmarks for each child. Change your page setup to landscape and use the label portion of your word processor.

- Create mailing labels to send letters home.

PLANTS AND THEIR PARTS

Show off the group and independent research that your students have done with this newsletter.

Grade Level: three to five

Duration: two hours layout and computer time

Materials: a newsletter program such as *Press Writer* or *Microsoft Publisher* (or a word processor such as *Microsoft Word* or *Works*), a computer drawing program such as *Paint* (or a scanner to capture paper drawings)

Electronic encyclopedias such as *World Book*, *Grolier*, *Encarta*, and *Infopedia* are good sources for information, as well as the student textbooks, library books, and "regular" encyclopedias.

Procedure: During the study of plant parts, groups can work together doing research on the various parts of a plant. The students can then write up their findings and produce a newsletter to share with others what they have learned.

Before the Computer:

- Decide who is going to perform each job. You will need researchers, writers, artists, editors, and layout designers.

- Research the appearances, functions of, and uses for roots, stems, leaves, seeds, flowers, etc.

- Drawings may be done on programs such as *Paint* or *Corel Draw*.

On the Computer:

- Using a newsletter program or a word processor that will allow you to format into columns, allow the students to design, lay out, type, proofread, and print the newsletters.

Internet Link:

- *http://www.fi.edu/tfi/units/life/*
  This site is called "Living Things." The "Individuals" section deals with anatomy and physiology of plants and animals. "Circle of Life" has life cycles of many plants and animals. It is maintained by the Franklin Institute Science Museum in Philadelphia, Pennsylvania.

PLANTS AND THEIR PARTS (cont.)

Sample Newsletter

Plants and Their Parts

December, 1999
Volume 1, Issue 1

Inside this issue

1 Roots Keep the Plant in Place

1 Stems Form the Frame

1 Leaves Manufacture the Food for the Plant

2 Seeds Make New Plants

Mrs. Kennedy's third grade class has been discussing how plants are designed and how each part of the plant does a different job to help the plant.

Roots Keep the Plant in Place

by Johnny

Roots are the parts of the plant that are in the ground. They keep the plant from washing away in the rain or blowing away in the wind.

Roots also take water and minerals from the soil to keep the plant healthy.

Different kinds of plants have different kinds of roots.

Some roots are long and go deep into the soil. Other plants have many little short roots that grow mostly above the ground.

Some food is stored iun the roots for use when food is scarce. Some roots are the part of the plant we eat, like carrots, potatoes, and radishes.

Stems Form the Frame

by Jim

The stems of plants hold up the leaves, flowers, and other parts of the plant that grow above the ground.

Stems are like straws. They let the leaves and flowers suck up water and minerals from the roots and also let food from the leaves go down to the roots.

Leaves Manufacture the Food for the Plant

by Amy

Leaves on plants get light from the sun, carbon dioxide from the air, and water from the soil and change it into sugar and oxygen. Leaves do this using chlorophyll, the chemical that makes leaves green.

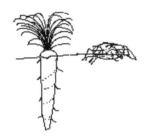

FLOWERING PLANTS

Discover the wildflowers growing in other parts of the world.

Grade Level: three to five

Duration: Actual computer time will vary depending on how many messages are sent and/or received. This activity will probably cover the flowering season in your part of the world but could extend to a year-round project.

Materials: a computer with a modem and access to e-mail, a digital camera or a regular camera, and a scanner (nice but not necessary to the success of the project).

Procedure: Gather information (and pictures, if possible) of your local and area wildflowers. Establish e-mail connections with other classes throughout the world in order to share and compare wildflowers.

Before the Computer:

- Learn what wildflowers grow in your area.

- Discuss and practice describing flowers clearly so that children across the world can get an accurate mental picture.

- Determine if you have the capability to send picture files through e-mail. If you don't, fear not! The project is sometimes more fun if you just describe the flowers.

- If you have access to a digital camera, become familiar with how to take pictures and save them in a format that you can send through your e-mail. If you have a scanner, become familiar with how to operate it and how to save picture files.

- It is better for the teacher to make contact with other teachers and groups before introducing the project to the students. Sometime it takes awhile to arrange correspondence with the other schools.

- Discuss with the students that different types of flowers grow in different ecosystems.

- Research with the students the wildflowers that grow in your area. Take (or collect) pictures, if convenient.

- Have the students write letters describing the wildflowers of your region: when they bloom, where they grow, the climate, the different types of flowers. Ask for information about wildflowers growing in the areas to which the students are writing.

On the Computer:

- Once an e-mail connection with other groups of children is established, send the messages from the students.

- Print the letters received from students across the world.

- Answer the messages received and, hopefully, establish a cultural exchange on several levels as well as learning about wildflowers.

FLOWERING PLANTS *(cont.)*

Related Activities:

- A database of wildflowers of the world would be an interesting way to record and interpret data from this project. Some possible fields are Scientific name, Local name, Location (country, region), Climate, Color, Number of petals, Month blooms appear, Type of leaf, Type of soil. I am sure you and your students can think of many more.

- Research myths and folklore associated with wildflowers. There are many stories associated with wildflowers. The students could make booklets of the stories they have heard from their parents, read in the library, and received from their e-mail friends.

- Make a collage of wildflower pictures from around the world. These could be received from e-mail friends or collected in other ways.

Internet Links:

- *http://www.epals.com/kpi.html*
  This page gives students an opportunity to meet and correspond with other classrooms from around the world.

- *http://www.ziplink.net/users/tlipcon/keypals/*
  This Web site will help you find a keypal in the country of your choice.

PLANT PROCESSES

Observe and measure the movement of water through a celery stalk.

Grade Level: five

Duration: one hour

Materials:

celery stalks about 8–10 inches long

clear plastic cup

food coloring

water

ruler

timer or clock

scissors

Procedure: Add 1 inch (2.5 cm) of water to the cup. Add food coloring to the water until the color is dark. Cut the bottom edge off of the celery, cut a notch in the stalk about 3 inches (8 cm) from the bottom, and place the stalk in the cup. Note the time. Observe the celery every 10 minutes. Measure the change in the color each time. After five observations, remove the celery from the water. Look for color changes above and below the notch. Cut the celery and observe the color.

Before the Computer:

- Do the experiment, stressing the importance of recording procedure and results.

- Discuss with the class whether using a chart to record data is more or less effective than a narrative.

- Be familiar with a word processing program that will allow you to draw tables. (*Word Perfect* and *Microsoft Word* both have this capability. I am sure there are others.)

On the Computer:

- Draw a chart using the table-drawing capabilities. It should include sections for time and color changes, final observations, and conclusions.

- Record, or have the students record, their observations of the experiment.

- Discuss the final conclusions and record them on the chart.

- Print the chart for the students to have for reference.

Internet Link:

- *http://plants.usda.gov/plants/*

PLANT PROCESSES *(cont.)*

Observing the Movement of Water Through Celery

Time	Color Changes

Total distance water moved:

Color change above notch?

Color change below notch?

Inferences and conclusions:

HOW ANIMALS GROW

Show the life cycles and characteristics of different animals

Grade Level: three

Duration: five to fifteen minutes a day

Materials: drawing program such as *Paint*; publishing program such as *The Print Shop*, *Microsoft Publisher*, *Print Artist*, *Printmaster Gold*   (There are many good ones.)

Procedure: The students will draw, import graphics, or otherwise depict the growth and other characteristics of different animals.

Before the Computer:

- Study the life cycles of different animals.

On the Computer:

- Choose categories (a class activity or teacher's choice). Some examples of categories are animals that fly, animals that run fast, animals whose babies look very different from their parents, animals whose babies look similar to their parents, animals that walk, animals that swim, animals that have hair, animals that have feathers, animals that have backbones, animals that have no backbones, animals that have scales, animals that have fur, animals that come from eggs, etc.

- Put the categories at the tops of the pages. Have the students draw and color, draw using a paint program, or create their own pages using the poster or sign creator in a desktop publishing program. The children will put on the pages pictures of animals that fit into the classifications at the tops of the pages.

- Use the pages to create a class book of animals divided into categories. I use a ring binder for this. The book always turns out to be bigger than I think it will and is enjoyed by the students on a daily basis as it is being created. If you have access to a laminator, it is a good idea to laminate the pages.

Internet Link:

- *http://netvet.wustl.edu/ssi.htm*
  This site has information about nearly every animal you can name.

HOW ANIMALS GROW (cont.)

HOW ANIMALS GROW *(cont.)*

Animals that Have Scales

ANIMAL BEHAVIOR

Keeping records is vital to any scientific study. In this lesson, the students practice keeping a journal while researching animal behavior.

Grade Level: five

Duration: two weeks

Materials: access to the Internet, encyclopedias (both electronic and books), local zoo, library books

Procedure: Each student (or group) will choose a group of animals to research, such as dogs, cetaceans, spiders, amphibians, etc. For each research session, the students will keep a journal of facts learned, impressions, inferences, and any other information they feel needs to be recorded. When the research is completed, the journal will provide an excellent set of notes from which to write a report. Research techniques and results can also be discussed and compared by trading journals with one another.

Before the Computer:

- Choose the type of animal to be studied.

- Determine what resources are available and how they are to be used (online time schedule, trips to the library, perhaps a field trip to the zoo).

On the Computer:

- The format for the journal pages should be decided upon and the blank journal pages printed before the actual project starts to save computer time. You may use a word processor or a desktop publishing program to create your journal page template. This journal may be kept on the computer, but generally it is better for the students to have the pages at hand to write on while they are doing their research.

- A good way to find information on a particular subject on the Internet is to use a search engine. There are many good ones available, such as Infoseek, WebCrawler, Excite, and Alta Vista. A site that will let you choose from many search engines is the Virtual Search Engine page located at *http://www.dreamscape.com/frankvad/search.html.*

- Have the students use the journal pages to record the time spent, the location of the information, and the notes taken.

- A folder or binder for the journal pages is very helpful.

- When the research is complete, a word processor can be used to produce the report.

- You can capture images simply by right-clicking (or holding the mouse button down if you have a Mac) on the image and saving it to disk. These are okay to use in student reports unless otherwise noted. However, you cannot use them commercially or in multiple copies without permission from the copyright holder.

ANIMAL BEHAVIOR *(cont.)*

Internet Links:

Here are some general animal behavior links as well as some specific ones that I found interesting. However, do not limit your students to sites someone else discovers. The joy of discovery and the excitement of the search are what make research an adventure that is fun for young and old alike.

General Animal Behavior:

- *http://www.ahandyguide.com/cat1/a/a808.htm*
  A wonderful list of links to almost anything you could think of concerning animals, this is one of my favorites.

- *http://www.tigerden.com/Animals/*
  This is an index to animal related sites.

- *http://netvet.wustl.edu/ssi.htm*
  The electronic zoo site has its links divided into categories, which makes research easier for students. It is a very comprehensive site; there are links to picture galleries and even animal sounds!

- *http://www.learner.org/content/k12/jnorth/*
  Journey North, a site dealing with wildlife migration, is interactive and quite informative.

Specific Animals:

- *http://ham.spa.umn.edu/kris/science.html*
  Not much serious research is here, but the site is entertaining and has just the sort of things fifth graders need to know in order to contribute to the dinner table conversation. For example, did you know a cockroach can live for nine days without its head?

- *http://www.seaworld.org/beluga_whales/befirst.html* (click on behavior)
  Whale behavior is discussed here.

- *http://www.nmmnh-abq.mus.nm.us/nmmnh/mammals.html*
  New Mexico mammals are listed here.

  http://www.im.nbs.gov/amphibs.html (click on Teachers' Toolbox)
  Amphibians are the subject of this site.

- *http://www.csu.edu.au/faculty/commerce/account/frogs/frog.htm*
  The somewhat amusing world of frogs is revealed here.

MY SCIENCE PROJECT JOURNAL

Name _____ Date _____

Location: (Internet address, name of book, encyclopedia, name of person interviewed, etc.)

_____

Facts learned:	
Inferences and impressions:	
Other interesting information:	

INSECTS

Learning about insects is always fun. This activity will let the students learn about insects in other parts of the world, as well as those in their own backyards.

Grade Level: three to five

Duration: several 30-minute sessions (Actual computer time can be very short—10 minutes for typing letters sent and printing letters received each day.)

Materials: access to the Internet, insect identification books, data sheets, World (or U.S. if you prefer) map

Procedure: After introducing the study of insects and talking about some of the different types of insects, hand out the data sheets (which you or some of your students made using a word processing program such as *Writing Center*, *Microsoft Word*, *Claris Works*, *The Print Shop*, *Print Artist*).

Ask the students to think about what insects they have seen in the neighborhood. You may want to have the students capture insects and bring them to class for observation. The containers can be wooden boxes with fine screening to deter escape or baby food jars with breathing holes in the lids. On the data sheets record the kind of insect, a description of it or a drawing, where it was found (grass, water, tree, bathroom, etc.) and any comments the children have about it (pretty, mean looking, really creepy, stings, tickles when it walks on you, etc.).

For one or two class sessions, if it is feasible, take the students on a collection walk. They can capture insects to take back to class or just observe them and add them to their data sheets. In the classroom, use the insect identification books to identify the insects and find out more about each one.

Before the Computer:

- Have the students write letters to other students, sharing with them the insects they found and some information about your school.

- It is a good idea to have the arrangements made for the exchange before you start the insect unit. There are many sites on the Internet for locating keypals and also several places that you can propose a project such as this one and have a much larger participation. Even if you put it on a project list, I would be sure to have a couple of groups that I was sure of. It is really disappointing to the children (and their teacher) if the response is sparse.

On the Computer:

- Explain to the students how e-mail works—that the computers use phone lines (usually) to send the letters electronically to other computers. E-mail stands for electronic mail. Show the students the commands for composing e-mail and for sending it.

INSECTS *(cont.)*

- Have the children type their letters into a word processing program and save them to upload to the e-mail provider, or type them directly into e-mail if you have multiple access.

- When answers are received from the other schools, post the letters on a bulletin board so that the students may record insects from the other locations on their data sheets.

- Use "dot" labels to mark on a map the locations from which you have insect lists. We combined this project with another class that was studying wildflowers. On a common map, we put bug stickers for the insect project and flower stickers for the flower project. The students enjoyed the more colorful stickers, which were inexpensive and easily found in a stationery store.

Internet Links:

- *http://www.ex.ac.uk/~gjlramel/front.html*
  An entomological page that is one of the best, it has links to "Insects—Order by Order," "The Insects Home Page," "Insect Anatomy," etc.—A must-see.

- *http://www.ex.ac.uk/bugclub/*
  This is a delightful site that has many fun activities to include in your study of insects. I have included a picture of a portion of this site simply to show you what is available.

- *http://www.epals.com/kpi.html*
  Some keypal links are available at this site.

- *http://www.wimmera.net.au/projects/projects.html*
  I really like this one for projects and connecting with other classes.

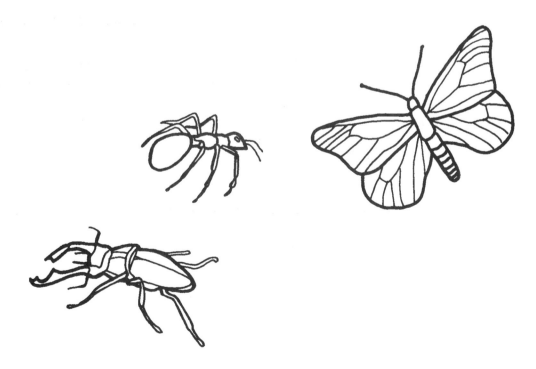

INSECTS *(cont.)*

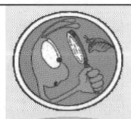

THE AES Bug Club
FOR YOUNG ENTOMOLOGISTS

NO FRAMES VERSION   AWARDS

RECENTLY UPDATED PAGES: Bug FAQ, Events, Links Section

Details of the 1998 AES Exhibition

Do you want to cuddle a Cockroach, stroke a Stick Insect or hug a Harvestman?

Do you find earthworms, beetles, bugs and other creepy crawlies fascinating or even exciting?

IF YOU DO THEN THE BUG CLUB IS FOR YOU?

The Bug Club navigation:
- The Bug Club
- Membership
- Newsletter
- Bug Pets
- Pen Pals
- Bug ID
- Books & Bugs

The Bug Club is a club devoted to young people and the "Young at heart" who find insects and other creepy crawlies interesting and even fascinating.

We publish a colourful **newsletter** six times a year packed with interesting articles, games, puzzles and fun things to do and make all related to creepy crawlies.

▪ We also organise a number of field events throughout the year. In the Summer we run Butterfly Walks, Spider Safaris, Pond Dips and many other exciting activities.

▪ In the Winter we have discovered "Where creepy crawlies go in the Cold Weather" and have been behind the scenes of the Natural History Museum in London.

Why not check out the UPDATED **Events Page** for Field Reports and Up & Coming events.

If you represent a School, College or other Professional Organisation then visit our **Education Section**.

Go to the Bug Club **Frequently Asked Questions** page.
IT IS NOW TIME TO RENEW YOUR MEMBERSHIP

INSECT DATA SHEET

Kind	Description (What does it look like?)	Location	Comments

VERTEBRATE SLIDE SHOW

A good culminating activity to a unit on vertebrates is a trip to the zoo. Take along a digital camera and make the trip live on.

Grade Level: three to five

Duration: varies with the number of slides

Materials: digital camera, planning sheets, any slide show program such as *Power Point* or *Kid Pix* (If you don't have a digital camera, you can take regular snapshots and use a scanner to convert them.)

Before the Computer:

- After finishing the unit on vertebrates, plan a field trip to the local zoo. Take along a digital camera or a regular camera. Use the planning sheets to plan what captions or audio narration will be used for each slide. Make sure that each student has the snaps he or she wants.

On the Computer:

- Download the pictures from the camera into the computer, or scan the photos and save to disk.

- Open the slide show program and load a photograph on each truck (*Kid Pix*) or frame and load a photograph for each slide in *Power Point*.

- Allow the students to add audio narration to each slide.

- Roll the credits, and you're ready to share your field trip with other classes, parents on open-house night, the school board, or next year's class.

Internet Links:

- *http://www.broderbund.com* (click on KidPix)
- *http://www.broder.com/education/programs/art/kidpix/newschool.html*
  information about *Kid Pix*

- *http://officeupdate.microsoft.com/index.htm#PowerPointdownloads*
  information about *Power Point*

- *http://www.cpb.uokhsc.edu/okc/okczoo/zoomap.html*
  If you can't visit a real zoo, try the above link.

- *http://www.mindspring.com/~zoonet/www_virtual_lib/zoos.html*
  Find links to over 100 different zoos.

SLIDE SHOW PLANNING SHEET

Name _____ Date _____

What my slide will show	*What I want to say about it*
Slide #	
Slide #	
Slide #	
Slide #	

LIVING THINGS NEED EACH OTHER

How better to learn that living thing need each other than to have a cooperative learning project? The students will research different ecosystems and produce a booklet showing the results of their efforts.

Grade Level: three to five

Duration: four or five sessions with planning, research, discussion, and publishing

Materials: encyclopedias (electronic or not), access to the Internet (optional), research guides, library books, a word processor such as *Children's Writing Center*, *Microsoft Word*, *Microsoft Publisher*

Procedure: The students will be divided into groups. They need to decide what needs to be researched, who will do the research on each topic, who will decide what to write, who will type, who will edit, what format their publication will be, and other topics.

Before the Computer:

- In a class discussion, have the students decide what is to be included in their publications on communities and ecosystems. They will need to be guided to see the interdependence of the organisms.

- Group the students and explain the interdependence of the members of this community. If there aren't enough researchers, the writers won't have enough to write. The students will see that it is not just food chains. In an ecosystem, there are many relationships.

On the Computer:

- Using the class choices, create a research guide and duplicate it for the researchers to use for recording data.

- Using the Internet search engines, encyclopedias, libraries, and resource persons, the researchers will gather data.

- After the groups have decided what needs to be included in the publication, the students will create their booklets.

- If the students choose to make half-page booklets, they need to decide how to position the pages in order for them to be in order in the booklet.

  Microsoft Publisher makes this relatively painless, especially if you have a printer that will format double-sided printing. Even if your printer doesn't, a little advance planning (and a few trial-and-error mistakes) will make you a pro. On "page setup" (found in the File menu) choose Special Fold, Book Fold, and change the orientation to Landscape.

  In *Microsoft Word*, you will need to choose Page Setup (found in the File menu) and choose Paper Size, and Landscape. Then when you are ready to type, choose Columns from the Format menu and divide your sheet into 2 columns. Each column will be a page in your booklet.

LIVING THINGS NEED EACH OTHER *(cont.)*

Press Writer by Brøderbund also has a booklet option that is very easy to use, as do several other programs.

Internet Links:

- *http://outcast.gene.com/ae/AE/AEPC/WWC/1991/biome_swap.html*
  This site is a report on a project which allows students to exchange information about different geographic biomes. There are excellent ideas here.

- *http://www.eduweb.com/amazon.html*
  At Amazon Interactive – explore the geography of the Ecuadorian Amazon through games and activities.

- *http://www.snowcrest.net/freemanl/geography/slides/biomes/*
  Internet resources on ecosystems, biomes, and animals reside here.

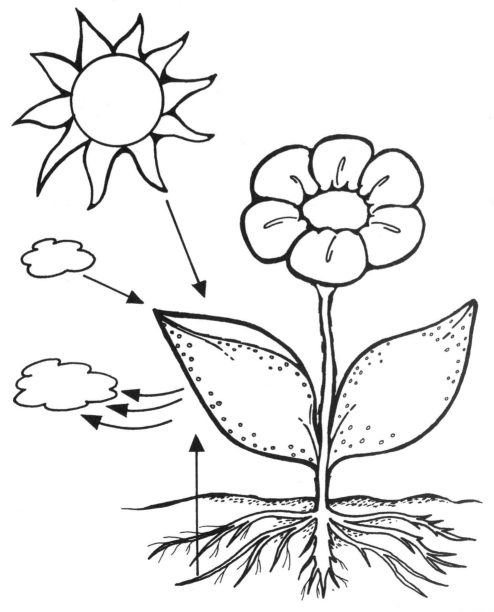

OUR ECOSYSTEM RESEARCH GUIDE

Group _____ Date _____

1. What type of ecosystem is it? (desert, ocean, estuary, lake, plains, forest, arctic) _____

   _____

   _____

   _____

   _____

   _____

2. What plants grow in this system? _____

   _____

   _____

   _____

   _____

   _____

3. What animals live in this system? _____

   _____

   _____

   _____

   _____

   _____

4. How are energy and materials acquired? _____

   _____

   _____

   _____

   _____

5. How does the system process its waste? _____

   _____

   _____

   _____

   _____

OUR ECOSYSTEM RESEARCH GUIDE *(cont.)*

6. What organisms help each other? How? _____

_____

_____

_____

_____

_____

7. What organisms compete for food?_____

_____

_____

_____

_____

_____

8. What organisms compete for space? _____

_____

_____

_____

_____

_____

9. What effect do you think this competition has on the ecosystem?_____

_____

_____

_____

_____

_____

_____

10. What other relationships did you discover? _____

_____

_____

_____

OUR ECOSYSTEM RESEARCH GUIDE *(cont.)*

11. What effect do you think these relationships have on the ecosystem? _____

_____

_____

_____

_____

_____

_____

_____

_____

_____

_____

_____

_____

_____

_____

_____

_____

_____

_____

_____

_____

_____

_____

_____

_____

_____

_____

OUR ECOSYSTEM RESEARCH GUIDE *(cont.)*

Producers	for	Consumers

HOW PEOPLE AFFECT PLANTS AND ANIMALS

To reinforce a study on the relationship of man and nature, the students will draw or write their ideas.

Grade Level: three

Duration: 15 minutes computer time for each student

Materials: a drawing program such as *Paint* or *Kid Pix*

Before the Computer:

- Discuss with the students the ways in which humans affect habitats.
- Be sure you discuss the helpful as well as the detrimental ways habitats are changed.

On the Computer:

- Have the students draw or write (or both) about some of the ways that man changes plant and animal habitats.
- Use a drawing program such as *Paint* or *Kid Pix*.
- Print the students' work and display it on a bulletin board. The students can create banners with a publishing program to entitle the display, "Be careful to preserve their habitats," "We make changes—try to make them for the better," or something else appropriate.

Internet Links:

- *http://www.blm.gov/education/arctic/manage.html*
  The ways man has changed the arctic are noted at this site.

- *http://www.blm.gov/education/great_basin/great_basin.html*
  This is a Bureau of Land Management site.

- *http://rbcm1.rbcm.gov.bc.ca/End_Species/index_es.html*
  "Endangered Species in Endangered Spaces"—This is a Canadian site that lists endangered plants and animals. The best thing about the site, I think, is the fact that it explains why each species is endangered.

HOW PEOPLE AFFECT PLANTS AND ANIMALS *(cont.)*

Don't pollute the river

It destroys the fish's home. And they can't live with us.

I am glad my home is safe and healthy and clean.

FOOD CHAINS AND FOOD WEBS

A good way to better understand food chains and food webs is with manipulatives. And the students can make their own.

Grade Level: three to five

Duration: varies, depending on how many computers you have

Materials: yarn or colored string, scanner, digital camera, Internet access, drawing program (You can use any or all of these.), index cards (Avery has perforated ones, three to a sheet, #5388) or card stock that you can cut into cards later, a program that will let you format it to print index cards (*The Print Shop Deluxe Ensemble III* will—almost any label program will—or you can use cardstock and any program that will let you divide the sheet into different sections.)

Procedure:

- Print out cards with pictures of producers, herbivores, carnivores, omnivores, and decomposers.

- Put magnetic tape or tacky putty on the back of each card.

- Have the students build their own food webs, discussing why each card should go where they put it. They can use the yarn to connect the cards.

Before the Computer:

- a study of food chains and webs

On the Computer:

- Scan, draw, import from the Internet, or download from a digital camera pictures of various organisms.

- Try to have a good selection of producers, herbivores, carnivores, omnivores, and decomposers.

- Decide how large you want your cards and divide your drawing screen into as many cards as will fit, or use a readymade card size.

Internet Links:

- *http://www.earthsky.com/1996/es960406.html*
  A good discussion of ocean food chains can be found here.

- *http://www.arts.ouc.bc.ca/geog/G111/4e.html*
  A food chain is outlined at this site.

- *http://www.fi.edu/tfi/units/life/*
  Bill Nye, the Science Guy, explains food webs.

ANIMAL AND PLANT ADAPTATIONS

Children will learn about adaptations that plants and animals have made in order to survive over the centuries. They will learn how to share this information through an interactive presentation.

Grade Level: three to five

Duration: 120 minutes computer time

Materials: a presentation program such as *HyperStudio* or *Power Point*

Procedure: Obtain pictures (scanned photographs, digital photographs from your zoo trip, drawings by the students).

Before the Computer:

- Discuss behaviors animals have developed in order to survive (hunting at night in the desert so the heat won't kill, migration, hibernation).

- Discuss physical adaptations plants have made in order to survive (poison, thorns, needles instead of leaves).

- Discuss physical adaptations animals have made in order to survive (thick layer of blubber on whales, very large ears on desert animals, sonar in bats).

- Be sure the children understand that these changes were not made in one generation. The surface dwelling fish in Antarctica weren't suddenly without hemoglobin in their blood so that they could swim down from Hawaii and survive in the cold near the South Pole.

- Divide into groups and choose the type of adaptation each group will become "experts" on.

On the Computer:

- Do what research you need or want to do on the computer, using electronic encyclopedias, search engines on the Internet, online libraries, etc.

- Open your presentation program and explain to the children how to insert pictures, sounds, and text.

- Be available for help, but don't instruct too much on anything but the technology. I have found that children this age adapt wonderfully to this type of program and come up with creative approaches to getting their ideas across that I would have never tried.

Internet Links:

- *http://muddcs.hmc.edu/~tbassett/adam/yellow.html*
  Find an article about plant adaptations in Yellowstone National Park.

- *http://www.bio.mq.edu.au/outreach/redirect.html*
  Australian mammals are discussed.

- *http://officeupdate.microsoft.com/index.htm#PowerPointdownloads*
  Here you can find information on the *Power Point* program.

ANIMAL AND PLANT ADAPTATIONS *(cont.)*

- *http://www.hyperstudio.com/noframes/download/index.html*
  Some stacks you can download for *HyperStudio* are available.

- *http://www.cuug.ab.ca:8001/~johnstos/hyperst.html*
  Review some sample stacks from students in Canada.

CLASSIFYING LIVING THINGS

Scientists classify things according to different systems. We can make a classification system for any group, based on identification keys.

Grade Level: five

Duration: 60–120 minutes online time

Materials: Internet access, classification charts, different animal identification books, wildflower identification manuals, insect identification

Procedure:

- Groups of students will create their own classification systems for the identification of frogs.

- After the frogs are all identified and classified, compare systems and discuss how the identifications vary with the different systems.

Before the Computer:

- Look at the identification books and notice what types of identification keys are used in classifying things.

- Look at several different classification systems. Notice that they are based on similarities and differences of certain characteristics.

- Some of the frog identification keys might be color, defense, environment, sound, size, and food. However, the students need to choose their own criteria.

On the Computer:

- Go out onto the Internet and enter "frog" into a search engine (obviously, if frogs are not your thing, you may choose another group of animals).

- Look at and read about all of the kinds of frogs you can find.

- Save pictures and data.

- Make up your own classification system and classify all the frogs you found.

Internet Links:

- *http://www.seaworld.org/tiger/sciclasstiger.html*
  Scientific classification of tigers can be found here.

- *http://155.187.10.12/projects/frogs/anbg-frogs.html*

- *http://www.csu.edu.au/faculty/commerce/account/frogs/frog.htm*

- *http://Moogie.dragonfire.net/FROG!/pix.htm*

- *http://206.156.13.85*

CLASSIFYING LIVING THINGS *(cont.)*

A sample system:

	Color	Defense	Environment	Sound	Size
Frog #1					
Frog #2					
Frog #3					
Frog #4					
Frog #5					
Frog #6					
Frog #7					
Frog #8					
Frog #9					
Frog #10					
Frog #11					
Frog #12					
Frog #13					

POPULATIONS AND COMMUNITIES

After studying populations and communities, give the students a creative break and see how well they transfer knowledge.

Grade Level: three to five

Duration: 60 minutes

Materials: a word processing program such as *Children's Writing Center*, a drawing program such as *Paint*, or a program like *Kid Pix*

Procedure: Have the students create their own populations and communities and write stories about these communities and populations.

Before the Computer:

Plan the story, using a storyboard or planning sheet. Remember the characteristics of a population and a community.

On the Computer:

- Type the stories.
- Illustrate the stories.
- Print the stories.

Internet Link:

- *http://www.thewildones.org/sfcEnv.html*
  This is a report of a similar project. Some of the stories are really clever.

POPULATIONS AND COMMUNITIES *(cont.)*

Story Planning Sheet

Name _____ Date _____

Story Setting	**Main Characters**
Problem	**Solution**

PROPERTIES OF MATTER

If you are interested in something, it is always nice to find a brochure that tells you all about it. In this activity, the children can make their own brochure about the stages of matter.

Grade Level: three

Duration: about 30 minutes computer time

Materials: brochure paper or plain paper, a word processing program, a teacher-made identification work sheet

Procedure: The students will make a brochure advertising the stages of matter.

Before the Computer:

- Students try to identify as many solids, liquids, and gasses as they can at home and at school. They can bring samples to school, and the class can discuss each one to see which category it fits.

    Solid: stays the same shape, stays the same size, can be touched, can be seen

    Liquid: flows, changes shape, may or may not be seen

    Gas: changes shape, very low density, cannot be seen, cannot be felt

- Each student fills out a work sheet and then the class can consolidate the lists.

- Determine a definition for matter and one each for liquid, solid, and gas.

- Compose a paragraph telling about the activity and what tests were used to determine the stages of the different objects.

On the Computer:

- Use a program that has special fold capabilities for brochures, such as *Microsoft Publisher*, *Press Writer*, *Printmaster Gold 3.0*, or you can use your regular word processor, such as *Microsoft Word*, *Microsoft Works*, or *ClarisWorks*. If your word processor doesn't have special formatting for brochures, just go into page setup and change to landscape orientation and three columns. It will work fine.

- Determine what will go on each fold. The title and a paragraph describing the activity should go on the fold that will be the front.

- On each of the inside folds, make a list of objects that fit into the stages of matter: solid, liquid and gas—one per fold.

- On another fold you might want to list the objects that can be made to go from one stage to another, like water, cheese, and metal.

Extension Activities:

- Besides classifying the objects as solid, liquid, or gas, the students could expand the list of objects whose states can change to include information about reversing the change. It is easy to re-freeze water after it has thawed, but after it has changed into a gas, how easily can you change it back?

PROPERTIES OF MATTER *(cont.)*

- Determine which objects have odors.

- Determine which objects conduct heat or cold.

- Determine if an object can be two stages at once. Discuss colloids.

Internet Links:

- *http://www.eecs.umich.edu/mathscience/funexperiments/agesubject/physicalsciences.html*
  Lots of physical science activities are sorted by levels: early elementary, later elementary, middle school, high school.

- *http://192.239.146.18/resources/Science/PSAM.html*
  Downloadable activity files here include "Definition of Matter," "Measurement of Mass," and about 30 others.

States of Matter Work Sheet			
Object	Solid	Liquid	Gas

PROPERTIES OF MATTER *(cont.)*

States and Properties of Matter

Matter is anything that has mass (weight) and takes up space. A property is something about matter that can be observed and tells you something about the matter, such as color, smell, and shape.

One of the properties of matter is its form or state. Three states of matter are liquid, solid and gas. A liquid has definite volume, but has not shape of its own. It changes its shape to fit the container it is in. A solid has a certain shape and volume of its own. A gas does not have a shape of its own or a certain volume. Many times, you cannot even see gas.

Inside this brochure you will find many things listed by the state of matter they are.

Investigations donce by Mrs. McMillin's 3rd Grade Class

MEASURING MATTER

Creating a spreadsheet that will calculate conversions from U.S. customary measurements to metric and back will teach the students how to design a spreadsheet and work with formulas, as well as producing a useful tool to use.

Grade Level: five

Duration: 30 minutes computer time

Materials: a spreadsheet program, formulas for converting measurements

Procedure: Create a spreadsheet that will convert customary U.S. measurements to metric, metric to customary, and Fahrenheit to Centigrade.

Before the Computer:

- Understand what a spreadsheet does.

- Locate formulas for converting measurements.

On the Computer:

- Open the spreadsheet program.

- Leave one column blank for entering numbers to convert.

- In the second column enter the units of measurement (inches, feet, etc.) you are converting from.

- In the third column type the word "equals" or use an equal sign. This may be difficult, as most spreadsheets use the "=" as an indicator that the following data is a formula. You will have to make the program recognize the sign as text. This is done differently in different programs. In some, you precede it by a quotation mark. In others you go to format, then cells, and then text. You should be able to find it in your manual under "numbers as text" or something similar.

- In the fourth column you will enter your formulas. Use the cell name of the cell in column one in your formula. For example, =A5*2.54 will convert whatever number is entered in cell A5 to centimeters in cell D5.

- In column five enter the units of measurements you are converting to.

- Enter column headings, borders, or whatever else will make your spreadsheet more attractive and easier to use.

Internet Link:

- *http://www.mplik.ru/~sg/transl/index.html*
  This interactive measurement converter will instantly convert units of measure.

MEASURING MATTER *(cont.)*

Sample of a conversion spreadsheet:

	A	B	C	D	E	F
1		**Metric Conversion**				
2						
3		**U.S. Customary to Metric**				
4						
5	1	inches	=	2.54	centimeters	
6	2	feet	=	0.6	meters	
7	7	yards	=	6.3	meters	
8	5	miles	=	8	kilometers	
9	4	square inches	=	26	square centimeters	
10	3	square feet	=	0.3	square meters	
11		square yards	=	0	square meters	
12		acres	=	0	hectares	
13		cubic feet	=	0	cubic meters	
14		cords	=	0	cubic meters	
15		quarts	=	0	liters	
16		gallons	=	0	liters	
17		ounces (avdp)	=	0	grams	
18		pounds	=	0	kilograms	
19		horsepower	=	0	kilowatts	

INVESTIGATING MATTER—
MAKING MODELS

Learning why we use models and designing our own can help us realize the benefits of models and review what we know about atoms.

Grade Level: three to five

Duration: 15–30 minutes computer time

Materials:

- a drawing program such as *Kid Pix* or *Paint*

- evaluation sheet

Procedure: After studying atoms and discussing the importance of models, the students will design and draw their own models using the approach that seems clear to them.

Before the Computer:

- Study atoms.

- Examine models, discussing the purpose of using models.

On the Computer:

- Research different kinds of atoms and their makeup. You may use the Internet. The site at *http://users.boone.net/yinon/default.html* is a good place to start. Using what they have learned about models and what they have learned about atoms, the students will design and produce a model of an atom.

- The students will choose what type of atom to model. (Oxygen, carbon, or sodium atoms are relatively easy, but some students will be more ambitious.)

Internet Links:

- *http://www.tannerm.com/* (click on Atoms and Elements)
  Advanced information about atoms is found here.

- *http://pdg.lbl.gov/cpep/startstandard.html*
  This is an interesting presentation of the atom.

- *http://pdg.lbl.gov/cpep/adventure_home.html*
  This is the larger project within which the previous presentation of the atom is set. The whole project is worth viewing by the students.

INVESTIGATING MATTER— MAKING A MODEL *(cont.)*

Thinking Questions Before You Start

1. What does the word "model" mean?
2. What models have you seen?
3. Did these models help you understand the subject they represented?
4. Why do we make models?
5. Why would anyone want a model of an atom?
6. How can having a model of an atom help us?

Evaluating Models	
1. What parts does this model have? Does it have enough parts? Does it have too many parts? Explain.	
2. How does this model represent the atom?	
3. How is this model very different from the atom?	
4. How could examining this model help us?	
5. How could examining this model give us a wrong idea?	
6. How could this model be improved?	
7. Why would the changes in question 6 make the model better?	

INVESTIGATING MATTER—
MAKING A MODEL *(cont.)*

Some atom models:

Thanks to The Contemporary Physics Education Project in cooperation with the U.S. Department of Energy.

http://pdg.lbl.gov/cpep/adventure_home.html

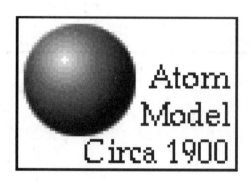

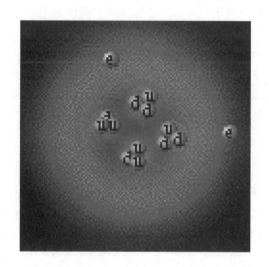

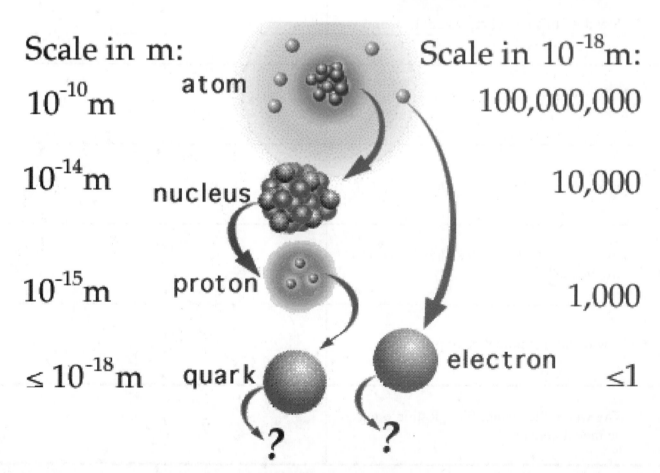

Scale in m: Scale in 10^{-18}m:

10^{-10}m   atom   100,000,000

10^{-14}m   nucleus   10,000

10^{-15}m   proton   1,000

$\leq 10^{-18}$m   quark   electron ≤ 1

?   ?

WORK AND MACHINES

Review is much more fun on the computer. This spreadsheet review is easy to construct, easy to use, and provides instant feedback.

Grade Level: three to five

Duration: 15 minutes teacher-time to create; 5–10 minutes per student to use

Materials: a spreadsheet program

Procedure: Create a spreadsheet for unit review.

Before the Computer:

- Become familiar with your spreadsheet program.
- Have a list of questions that can be answered with one or two words.

On the Computer:

- Open a spreadsheet document.
- Put an appropriate title on the spreadsheet
- Change columns and rows to the desired size.
- In the first column, enter the numbers for your questions.
- In the second column, enter the questions.
- Leave the third column blank, but widen it enough for the students to type answers.
- In the fourth column, use if/then statements to give feedback. For example:
  =If (C4="fulcrum","Great Answer!","Sorry, try again.")
  See the example on the next page.

Internet Link:

- *http://www.beakman.com/lever/lever.html*
  "How do levers make you stronger?"

WORK AND MACHINES *(cont.)*

Example of spreadsheet review:

Work and Machines Review

		Enter your answers below.	**Check your answers.**
1.	A lever turns on a point called a___.	fulcrum	Good job!
2.	All objects that have _____ can do work.	energy	Good job!
3.	A seesaw is a _____.	wheel and axle	Sorry, try again.
4.	A pencil sharpener is an example of a _____.	screw	Good job!
5.	The blade of a knife is an example of a _____.	wedge	Good job!
6.	Gravity is one kind of _____.	fulcrum	Sorry, try again.
7.	A _____is made of a wheel and rope.		Sorry, try again.
8.	A bicycle is a _____machine.		Sorry, try again.
9.	A _____has jagged edges like teeth.		Sorry, try again.
10.	There are six different _____.		Sorry, try again.
11.	Friction causes _____.		Sorry, try again.
12.	A ramp is an example of an _____.		Sorry, try again.

WORK AND MACHINES *(cont.)*

Spreadsheet screen, showing formula for cell D3:

D3		=	=IF(C3="fulcrum","Good job!","Sorry, try again.")

Workbook1

	A	B	C	D
1			Work and Machines Review	
2			**Type your answers below.**	**Check your answers.**
3	1	A lever turns on a point called a _____.	fulcrum	Good job!
4	2	All objects that have _____ can do work.	energy	Good job!
5	3	A seesaw is a _____.	wheel and axle	Sorry, try again.
6	4	A pencil sharpener is an example of a _____.	screw	Good job!
7	5	The blade of a knife is an example of a _____.	wedge	Good job!

FORMS OF ENERGY

Creating an interactive slide show to illustrate the various forms of energy will help the children understand it better.

Grade Level: three to five

Duration: 60–120 minutes

Materials: a presentation program like *Power Point* or *HyperStudio*, planning sheet, scanner, digital camera, clip art disks, drawing program (These last four are nice to have but are by no means essential for this activity.)

Procedure: Create an interactive slide show about the forms of energy. This activity lends itself well to cooperative learning groups. Each group could study a form of energy and become "experts." After the activity is finished, the "experts" would be available for assistance when the presentation was being used.

Before the Computer:

- Divide the students into cooperative learning groups.

- Assign or have each group choose a form of energy.

- The groups will study the forms of energy and plan the slides for their sections of the presentation.

- Each group will need to collect pictures to scan, find clip art, draw pictures, and/or take pictures with a digital camera to provide graphic illustrations for the slides.

- A teacher-made planning sheet is helpful to guide the children, but encourage them to be creative.

- It might be helpful to have some "jump-off" topics to help with the research:

    How does electrical energy affect our lives?

    How are electricity and magnetism related?

    What are some common devices for heating?

    What are some sources for heat energy?

    How can heat energy be conserved?

    What is noise pollution?

    How can sound energy be changed to other forms of energy?

    What are some man-made light sources?

    How would our lives be different if we had less sunlight? more sunlight?

    What parts of the human body have potential energy?

    What is the difference in potential energy and kinetic energy?

    Name some kinds of mechanical energy.

    What are six kinds of simple machines?

    What kinds of energy am I using when I mix the batter for a cake?

FORMS OF ENERGY *(cont.)*

On the Computer:

- Learn the skills necessary to use the presentation program.

- Each group will make its section of slides for the presentation, and then the teacher or another learning group will combine them.

- The presentation can be as simple or complex as you want it to be, depending on the skill level and creativity of your students. One third-grade group I worked with made a presentation of over 100 slides—each one interactive in several ways—including games and quizzes for evaluation.

- The opening screen should have buttons leading to each section.

Internet Links:

- *http://officeupdate.microsoft.com/index.htm#PowerPointdownloads*
  On the *Power Point* home page you can download a viewer program so that computers that do not have the *Power Point* program can still see your presentations. There are also templates and graphics and ideas for presentations here.

- *http://einstein.cs.uri.edu/tutorials/csc101/powerpoint/ppt.html*
  A complete online course for learning and using Power Point sponsored by the Department of Computer Science at the University of Rhode Island.

- *http://www.sasked.gov.sk.ca/docs/elemsci/gr4ubesc.html*
  A teaching unit on forms of energy from Saskatchewan, Canada can be found at this site.

- *http://www.zetnet.co.uk/sea.jnp/enfor1.htm*
  At this site you will find lesson plans on energy and forces.

FORMS OF ENERGY *(cont.)*

Planning Guide

Slide #

Buttons-links: _____

_____

_____

_____

Comments: _____

_____

_____

_____

Slide #

Buttons-links: _____

_____

_____

_____

Comments: _____

_____

_____

_____

Slide #

Buttons-links: _____

_____

_____

_____

Comments: _____

_____

_____

_____

Slide #

Buttons-links: _____

_____

_____

_____

Comments: _____

_____

_____

_____

FORMS OF ENERGY *(cont.)*

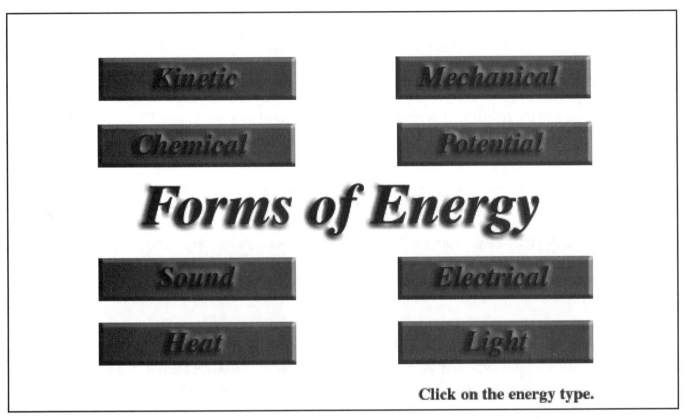

Click on the energy type.

Slide 1 Each word surrounding the title is a hidden button leading to the corresponding section.

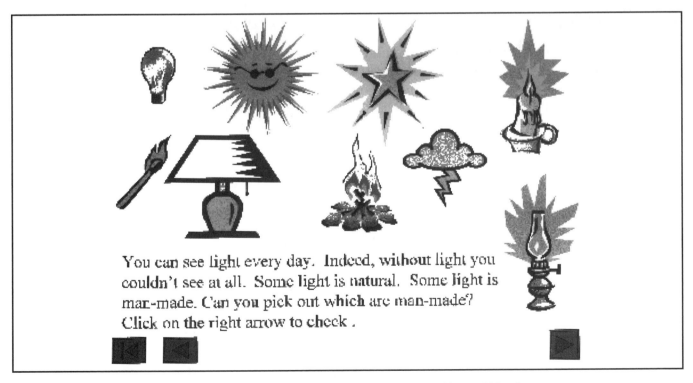

You can see light every day. Indeed, without light you couldn't see at all. Some light is natural. Some light is mar-made. Can you pick out which are man-made? Click on the right arrow to check .

This the first link from the word "Light" on slide 1.

SOUND

Take your students on a virtual field trip through the world of sound.

Grade Level: five

Duration: 15 minutes to several days, depending on how many side trips you take

Materials: access to the Internet (It is nice to have a screen projector or a large TV to make viewing the screen easier for the students. If you do not have access to these, you might want to do this activity with small groups.)

Procedure: Take the students through several interactive, fun, and informative sites that will help them learn about sound and sound waves. Also download the *Cthugha* program for exploring later.

Sounds surround us constantly, although we are frequently unaware of them. The children will discover that all sounds—even the ones they can't hear—are made of vibrations. They will learn how these vibrations are measured and interesting ways they are used.

Before the Computer:

- Before you do this or any online lesson with the children, it is a good idea to visit all of the sites yourself. Sometimes sites that were there yesterday are gone today. Also, if you explore the site yourself by yourself, you will not get any uncomfortable surprises with a classroom full of children watching.

- Keep a notebook for interesting sites that you want to visit later.

On the Computer:

- *http://nyelabs.kcts.org/nyeverse/episode/e12.html*
  Start your field trip with a visit to Bill Nye, the Science Guy. Bill Nye introduces you to sound waves and how your ears hear. He gives you some fun fast facts to carry with you and an experiment to try later. There are also library book suggestions to help you learn more about sound.

Episode 12

SOUND

SOUND *(cont.)*

- *http://www.li.net/~stmarya/stm/home.html*
  Here we find "Great Contributions" to the world of sound, such as Galileo, DaVinci, and Sir Isaac Newton. Also discussed is how sound is used in medicine, industry, science, and consumer goods. Dangers associated with sound and some precautions you should take are here.

- *http://www.exploratorium.edu/exhibits/vocal_vowels/vocal_vowels.html*
  How the shape of the vocal mechanism helps form the vowel sounds is the subject of our third stop. This is an exhibit at the Exploratorium in San Francisco, California. The Exploratorium is "a museum of science, art, and human perception with over 650 interactive 'hands on' exhibits." The exhibit shows how a duck call blown through differently shaped resonant chambers produces the vowel sounds. The students can hear the sound of the duck call and also the way the sound changes when the chamber is shaped differently. You really should bookmark this site and come back to it later. There are many exhibits to explore here.

- *http://www.nmns.edu.tw/CtrLife/eng1e.html*
  Here we find an article about sounds in nature from the National Museum of Natural Science in Taiwan. On their home page are many other science subjects.

- *http://www.ornl.gov/ornl94/blasting.html*
  From China, let us journey to New Mexico in the southwestern U.S.A. Here we find a story about how sound waves were used to locate the world's longest dinosaur skeleton.

- *http://www.explorescience.com/*
  Another fun and informative stop on our outing is the Explore Science with Shockwave page. You will need to download the Shockwave plug-in if you do not already have it (from *http://www.macromedia.com/shockwave/download*). You can watch sound waves from a moving source, demonstrating the Doppler effect, with or without interference patterns.

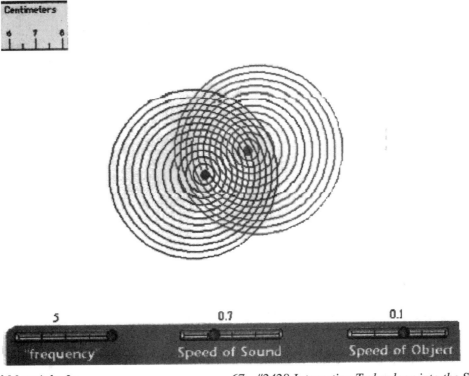

SOUND *(cont.)*

- *http://38.248.229.6/ss7x7/*
  Play with sound control just like a disc jockey! At the above site you will find the Wavestick 787.

- *http://www.afn.org/~cthugha/archives.html*
  For the final stop on our field trip, we go to the souvenir shop. Download *Cthugha* to explore offline in your classroom. *Cthugha* is an oscilloscope type of program that will take input from your audio CD or a microphone and display it as a colorful representation. It is well worth the time it takes to download it. *Cthugha* is available for downloading free at the above site. Go down the page until you see "Current Releases" and click on the one that applies to your operating system.

Note:

- The main page to *Cthugha* is *http://www.afn.org/~cthugha* but the descriptions may not be appropriate for your fifth graders to read.

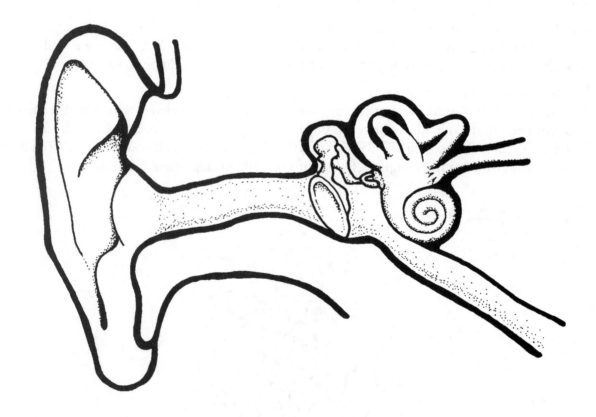

WORK AND ENERGY

Use your Web page editor to make in-class drills.

Grade Level: three to five

Duration: 15 or 20 minutes

Materials: a Web page editor such as *Netscape Gold, AOL Press, Claris HomePage* (*HyperStudio* or *Power Point* will work for this activity as well.)

Procedure: Make a self-checking drill for re-enforcement and learning. This is more fun than study sheets, and the students learn programming skills as well as the science lesson while creating drills.

Before the Computer:

- Each child (or group) needs to have a list of questions or scenarios and solutions.

- Some explanation needs to be done on the computer program you will be using.

On the Computer:

- Open the editor. Web page editors do not have to be connected to the Internet to design, create, or use the pages.

- On page one, introduce the subject and link to the questions. Each question (or group of questions) needs to be on a separate page.

- Make sure each question is linked to an answer page.

- Make sure there are links back to the question pages and to the main page. Dead ends are frustrating.

- Save the programs for use by other children. You will build an extensive library of drills on different subjects, which are great for studying for exams, after-school tutorial sessions, or study groups.

Internet Links:

- *http://www.swifty.com/apase/charlotte/energy.html*
  A study of energy is here.

- *http://www.col-ed.org/cur/sci/sci170.txt*
  Here you can find potential and kinetic energy activities dealing with downhill skiing and Olympic events.

- *http://www.col-ed.org/cur/sci/sci193.txt*
  Roller coasters in the classroom—this is a study of potential and kinetic energy.

WORK AND ENERGY *(cont.)*

Work Sheet

Questions	Answers

Title Page

Work and Energy

Choose your drill.

Question group 1

Question group 2

Question group 3

WORK AND ENERGY *(cont.)*

Group 1 Question Page

Work and Energy

Question Group 1

Decide whether or not any net work is being done, then click on the underlined question to check your answer.

1. John Kniffen is pushing against the side of his Dad's tractor, but the tractor doesn't budge. Is work being done on the tractor?

2. Jared Loper hits a home run in the baseball game. Is any work done on the baseball?

3. Russell Cozart is riding in his new red Corvette at 80 mph. Is the car doing any work on Russell?

4. Mr. Gilmore picks up a wrench from the workbench and holds it out at chest level. The wrench is not moving before or after this action. Is Mr. Gilmore doing any work on the wrench?

5. Mrs. Wright takes a book from the shelf in the library. Is any work being done on the book?

Go to Question Group 2

Go to Title Page

Answer Page for Group 1, Question 1

Group 1 - Question 1

No work is being done on the tractor.

If the tractor did not move, there was no work done.

Go on to the next question in this group.

Go back to Question Group 1

Go back to the Title Page

Go on to Question Group 2

ELECTRICITY AND MAGNETISM

Writing is exciting when you can do your research on the computer and make the final report attractive with word processing.

Grade Level: three to five

Duration: one hour for research, 30 minutes for typing

Materials: You will need a word processing program such as *Microsoft Works*, *Microsoft Word*, *ClarisWorks*, *Children's Writing Center*, or *Word Perfect*. Electronic or other encyclopedias will be helpful, as will library books and time on the Internet for research. A research guide is good for organization.

Procedure: Choose a scientist that did work in the field of electricity and magnetism. Research this scientist's life and work and share your research by publishing a report for others to read.

Before the Computer:

- Discuss some history of scientific exploration and the men and women involved.

- Each child (or group) may choose a scientist to study.

- Do the research and organize thoughts and information.

On the Computer:

- Do some research online or use an electronic encyclopedia if you have computer time available.

- After using a research guide to organize the report, type and illustrate reports on these scientists.

- Display the final reports in the library or on the "brag table" in the computer lab for others to share.

Internet Links:

- *http://www.mos.org/sln/toe/history.html*
  Van de Graaff's generator is the focus of this site.

- *http://www.mos.org/sln/toe/kite.html*
  Benjamin Franklin's kite experiment and St. Elmo's Fire are this site's subjects.

- *http://sln.fi.edu/franklin/rotten.html*
  Even more about Ben Franklin can be found here.

- *http://nisc8.upenn.edu/AR/men/bf.html*
  This site contains a biography of Benjamin Franklin.

- *http://www.ri.ac.uk/History/M.Faraday/*
  All you want to know about Michael Faraday is the content of this site.

- *http://minot.com/~mps/edison/edison/edison.html*
  The story of Thomas Edison can be found here.

ELECTRICITY AND MAGNETISM *(cont.)*

Research Guide

Name of Scientist:

Birth/Death:

Discoveries, theories, inventions:

Biographical information:

Other interesting notes:

Where I found my information:

ELECTRICITY AND MAGNETISM *(cont.)*

Cover Pages for Reports

My Report on Benjamin Franklin

by Bobbie Meixner

Thomas Alva Edison's electric light

by Pat Parker   *and Bob Smith*

LIGHT 1

Making a pinhole camera demonstrates how light travels in rays, as well as giving the students the basic elements of photography. The children will be justifiably proud of the pictures they can take with a camera they built themselves.

Grade Level: three to five

Duration: The research probably will take 15–30 minutes. The actual construction of the cameras will also take about 15–30 minutes.

Materials: access to the Internet or a trip to the library, a word processing program to record the results of the project

Procedure: Build pinhole cameras several different ways. Compare the results and discuss the reasons for the differences.

Before the Computer:

- Discuss the properties of light and how light travels from a light source in straight lines called rays.

- Before doing research and before the students begin constructing their cameras, I like to build one with wax-paper film to explain why the image is inverted.

Hint:

- I use a coffee can. Poke a hole in the center of the bottom of the can. Remove the can lid and put wax paper over the open end. (Use a rubber band or cellophane tape to hold it.) Keep the wax paper as smooth and tight as you can. Find a window with a bright sunny view. Set the can down with the hole pointing out the window. Make a tube of black paper about 12 inches long to shield the wax paper from the light. Press your face against the shield to view the images on the wax paper, or cover your head and the part of the coffee can nearest you with a large dark blanket or cloth. Be sure you stay about a foot away from the wax paper. Move the can until it is pointing at an object out in the sunshine. You will see a picture of the object on the wax paper—small and upside down.

On the Computer:

- Research on the Internet the properties of light and how to build a pinhole camera.

- At the bottom of this activity there are several locations on the Internet where I found more activities and articles on the properties of light.

- There are many sites dealing with pinhole cameras, what they do, how to build them, and galleries of pictures taken with them. I have listed a few here, but you can find more by using a search engine.

- *http://www.kodak.com/global/en/consumer/education/lessonPlans/pinholeCamera/*
  You can find instructions for building a cartridge camera and a can or box camera here.

- *http://www.exploratorium.edu/light_walk/camera_todo.html*
  Another good site for making a pinhole camera is here.

LIGHT 1 *(cont.)*

- At *http://photo.net/photo/pinhole/pinhole.htm*
  History, images, cameras, and formulas can be found here.

- After constructing and using your cameras, you will want to write up how the cameras were made, the different types of cameras, how pinhole cameras work, and the comparisons of the pictures made with the different types of pinhole cameras.

Options:

A nice touch would be to scan the photographs and add them to the school Web site to share with others.

Internet Links:

- *http://www.eecs.umich.edu/mathscience/funexperiments/agesubject/lessons/ftoptics.html*
  A lesson plan on how light travels is at this site.

- *http://www.eecs.umich.edu/mathscience/funexperiments/agesubject/lessons/prism.html*
  Here you can find a lesson plan on making prisms and separating light.

- *http://www.kie.berkeley.edu/KIE/web/hf.html*
  This is a full project on how far light goes. It is a debate on which of two theories is accurate: that light dies out the farther it gets from its source, or that light will go on forever if it is not absorbed. It gives the students experience in data gathering, interpreting data, and forming conclusions. An excellent project!

Some Thinking Questions:
What would happen to the image if you
changed the pinhole size?
colored the inside of the box black?
colored the inside of the box white?
used a longer or shorter box?
moved the camera closer to the subject?
moved the camera farther from the subject?
left the pinhole uncovered longer?
left the pinhole uncovered less time?
My own thinking questions:

LIGHT 1 *(cont.)*

A pinhole camera made
from a can

A pinhole camera made
from a box

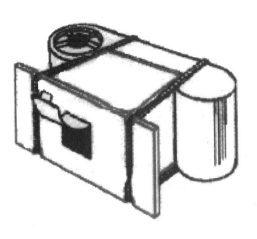

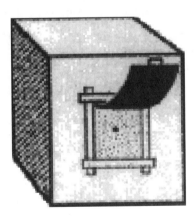

A cartridge pinhole camera

LIGHT 2

Visible light consists of bands of light. Red, orange, yellow, green, blue, indigo, and violet can be seen if we separate the visible spectrum into its parts.

Grade Level: three

Duration: 15 minutes

Materials: a paint or drawing program, a glass of water, a sheet of white paper, a sheet of dark construction paper, scissors, tape, and a clear drinking glass full of water

Procedure: Light is made up of waves—some waves move and oscillate faster or slower than others. When these waves hit water, they bend or refract differently, separating white light into its colors.

Before the Computer:

- Explain to the children about white light being made up of waves which we see as colors.

- Have the children cut a piece of construction paper the same height as the glass and about four inches (10 cm) wider.

- Cut a vertical slit in the center of the construction paper about ¹/₂ inch (1.3 cm) wide, extending from about ¹/₂ inch (1.3 cm) from the top to about ¹/₂ inch (1.3 cm) from the bottom. Tape the construction paper to the glass.

- Put the glass in the sun or have a light source to shine on it through the slit in the construction paper.

- Place the white paper in front of the glass.

- Have the children observe the bands of color on the paper.

On the Computer:

- Have the children draw and color the bands of color that were on the paper.

- Research some of Sir Isaac Newton's experiments and have the children illustrate them using the drawing program.

Internet Links:

- *http://www.bena.com/lucidcafe/library/95dec/newton.html*
  Information about Sir Isaac Newton is at this site.

- *http://www.orst.edu/~forsterp/optic.html*
  You may need to paraphrase this for your third graders, but it is a very interesting article.

- *http://cse.ssl.berkeley.edu/light/light_tour.html*
  An interactive unit on light can be found here.

LIGHT 2 *(cont.)*

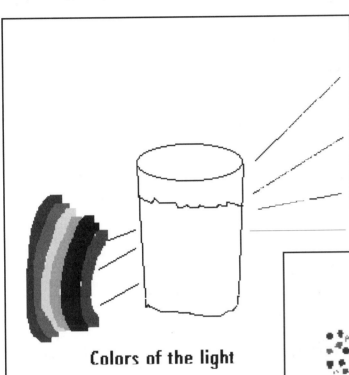

Colors of the light

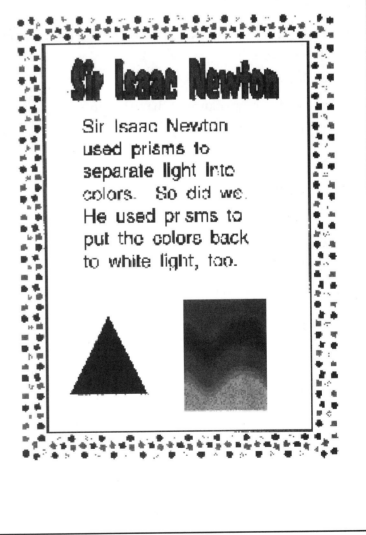

Sir Isaac Newton

Sir Isaac Newton used prisms to separate light into colors. So did we. He used prisms to put the colors back to white light, too.

HEAT AND MATTER

Measure the cooling rates of different volumes of water.

Grade Level: three to five

Duration: 20 minutes for experiment and recording data, 15 minutes computer time for setting up spreadsheet and graph

Materials:

- four jars of varying sizes (I use a baby food jar, a pint jar, a quart jar, and a gallon jar.)
- hot water
- four thermometers
- clock or watch with second hand
- record sheet (I used the *Microsoft Word* tables feature for mine.)
- spreadsheet program

Procedure:

- Fill all jars with hot water, recording the temperature of each at the time. (They should be the same.)
- Leave the thermometers in the jars.
- Record the temperature of the water in each jar every minute for 15 minutes.

Before the Computer:

- Fill in the data sheet.

On the Computer:

- Open the spreadsheet program.
- Assign rows for each time period.
- Assign columns for the temperature of each jar.
- Assign a final column for the difference in temperature between the smallest and largest jars.
- Enter a formula to compute the differences.
- Import the spreadsheet data to a word processing program as a line graph.

Internet Links:

- *http://science.cc.uwf.edu/sh/curr/heat/heat.htm*
  A good definition of heat can be found here.

- *http://www.hcc.hawaii.edu/hccinfo/instruct/div5/sci/sci122/newton/heat/heattemp.html*
- *http://www.hcc.hawaii.edu/hccinfo/instruct/div5/sci/sci122/newton/heat/sphtmass.html*
  Heat loss or gain in relation to mass is covered at these sites.

HEAT AND MATTER *(cont.)*

Record Your Results					
	Temperatures				
	Jar 1	**Jar 2**	**Jar 3**	**Jar 4**	**(Jar 4 – Jar 1)**
0 minutes					
1 minute					
2 minutes					
3 minutes					
4 minutes					
5 minutes					
6 minutes					
7 minutes					
8 minutes					
9 minutes					
10 minutes					
11 minutes					
12 minutes					
13 minutes					
14 minutes					
15 minutes					

HEAT AND MATTER *(cont.)*

	A	B	C	D	E	F
1	Heat Loss in Different Volumes of Water					
2						difference between jars 1 & 4
3		Jar 1	Jar 2	Jar 3	Jar 4	
4	0 minutes	200	200	200	200	0
5	1 minutes	195	190	185	180	15
6	2 minutes	190	180	170	160	30
7	3 minutes	185	170	155	140	45
8	4 minutes	180	160	140	120	60
9	5 minutes	175	150	125	100	75
10	6 minutes	170	140	110	80	90
11	7 minutes	165	130	95	70	95
12	8 minutes	160	120	80	70	90
13	9 minutes	155	110	70	70	85
14	10 minutes	150	100	70	70	80
15	11 minutes	145	90	70	70	75
16	12 minutes	140	80	70	70	70
17	13 minutes	135	70	70	70	65
18	14 minutes	130	70	70	70	60
19	15 minutes	125	70	70	70	55

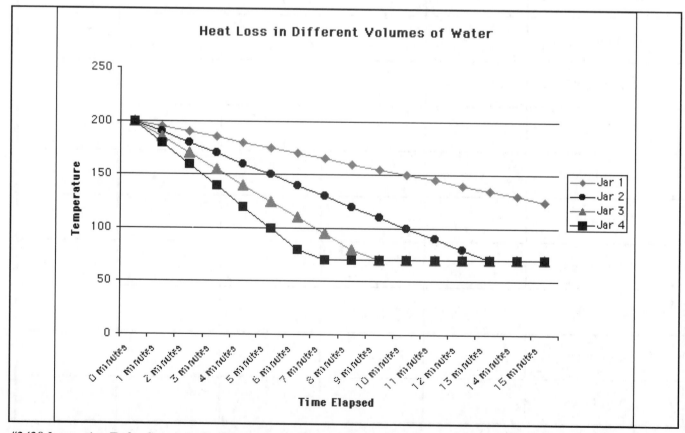

CHANGING FORMS OF ENERGY

Energy is defined as the "ability to do work." In this activity, the groups of children will share with others their discoveries about how energy can be changed from one form to another.

Grade Level: four to five

Duration: one class period per group for research; at least one class period for discussion, organization, and producing; probably two class periods (depending on the size of your class) for presentation

Materials: access to the Internet, encyclopedias (electronic or paper), library books, presentation programs, word processing programs, drawing programs, research sheet

Procedure: Energy can change forms. Your body changes the energy in food into energy you can use to do things. Wind-powered generators turn the energy in the wind into electrical energy to power our homes. Sonograms change sound energy into electrical energy and then into light signals that we can see to look inside our bodies without damaging them. Explore some of these energy changes and report the findings to the class in various ways.

Before the Computer:

- Divide the class into cooperative learning groups.

- Have each group choose a changing form of energy to study.

- Brainstorm research techniques and presentation ideas.

On the Computer:

- Use the Internet for research. Use your search engines to look for information. Some search engines can be found at these URLs:

>   Alta Vista—*http://www.altavista.com*
>   Excite—*http://www.excite.com*
>   Findspot—*http://www.findspot.com*
>   Galaxy—*http://www.einet.net/galaxy.html*
>   Hotbot—*http://www.hotbot.com*
>   Infoseek—*http://www.infoseek.com*
>   Lycos—*http://www.lycos.com*
>   Magellan—*http://www.mckinley.com*
>   MetaCrawler—*http://www.metacrawler.com*
>   Open Text—*http://www.opentext.com*
>   WebCrawler—*http://webcrawler.com*
>   Yahoo!—*http://www.yahoo.com*

CHANGING FORMS OF ENERGY *(cont.)*

- Use regular or electronic encyclopedias such as *Infopedia*, *Encarta*, *World Book*, or *Grolier* for research.

- Some library books on the subject of energy include

  Energy (Millbrook Press) by Larry White

  The Oxford Children's Book of Science, American Edition, by Charles Taylor and Stephen Pople

  Matter (Eyewitness Science) by Christopher Cooper

  Electricity and Magnetism (Usborne Understanding Science) by Peter Adamczyk, Paul-Francis Law, Andy Burton (illustrator), E. Humberstone

  Energy (Science Horizons) by Robert Snedden

  Energy and Power by R. Spurgeon

- After doing the research, design and create your presentation. The groups may do slide shows using *Kid Pix*, *HyperStudio*, or *Power Point*. They may do a written report with illustrations. Oral reports with visual aids are very effective.

Internet Links:

- *http://www.studyweb.com*
  This is a comprehensive site for doing research on nearly any subject.

- *http://nyelabs.kcts.org/nyeverse/episode/e45.html*
  Bill Nye, the Science Guy has some interesting "energy" experiments. Check out the kinetic and chemical energy changes at the above site.

The California Energy Commission has an amazing site. One of its many features is projects. Go to the following URL and then click on the project titles below that would work well with this lesson. *http://www.energy.ca.gov/energy/education/projects/projects-html/projects.html*

- *Peanut Power*
  changing stored energy to chemical energy

- *Battery Life—A Science Experiment*
  demonstrating which battery lasts longer

- *Lemon Power*
  changing chemical energy to electrical energy, making a voltaic battery to power a digital watch

- *Make Your Own Lightning*
  making mini-lightning bolts to see how lightning works in a storm

- *Using Water to Produce Energy*
  using the potential energy of moving water to produce mechanical energy to produce electrical energy

- *Make a Steam-Powered "Rocket Boat"*
  using the energy produced when water changes to steam to move a boat

CHANGING FORMS OF ENERGY *(cont.)*

My Energy Research	
What I learned	**Where I found it**

CHANGING FORMS OF ENERGY *(cont.)*

The students can design and create special paper for their reports.

ENERGY RESOURCES

Turn your class members into newscasters and filmmakers with a documentary or a newscast about the various energy resources: where they are found, how they are made usable, how expensive they are to refine or produce, whether they are renewable, etc.

Grade Level: three to five

Duration: two 45-minute class periods for non-computer brainstorming, organization, planning, practice, and scriptwriting

Materials: a video camera, access to the Internet and/or library, research sheets (The research sheet reproducible for "Changing Forms of Energy" will work fine for this project.)

Procedure: Produce your own documentary about Energy Resources. Working with video is highly motivational and encourages cooperative learning by working on a production crew. The research of the subject, the writing of the script, and the practices ensure that the students will learn the subject thoroughly.

Before the Computer:

- The teacher needs a basic knowledge of video production. You also need to be familiar with the particular camera that your students will be using.

- If this is your first class video project, you will need to spend a class period explaining camera use, strategies, and rules.

- Talk about documentaries. Most of the children have viewed many of them on the Discovery Channel, The Animal Planet, PBS, National Geographic, and other television channels and programs.

- Discuss news programs. Local newscasts and national newscasts are handled somewhat differently from a program like CNN produces. News programs such as *20/20* and *Eye on America* are another type. *Good Morning America* and the *Today* show are also types of news programs.

- Have the students view some of these types of television programs at home if they can. Encourage them to make notes about how the programs were handled.

- Each group will choose an energy resource to research and have as the subject of their video.

- Think and discuss in groups the types of questions that need to be answered about energy resources and whether they will do a documentary or a newscast.

- Do non-computer research in the library or use encyclopedias.

On the Computer:

- Research the subjects on the Internet, or use electronic encyclopedias, or both. I found quite a bit of information on geothermal energy, fossil fuels, hydropower, ocean energy, nuclear energy, solar energy, biomass energy, and wind energy using only the two sites in the "Internet Links" section of this activity.

ENERGY RESOURCES *(cont.)*

After the Research:

- Using their notes, the students will write scripts for their video. It is advisable to set a time frame to shoot for because some will think 30 seconds is plenty, and others will want to produce a mini-series.

- Organize practice sessions before the actual filming. This project requires much planning and organization and still will occasionally disintegrate into chaos. Expect it; plan on how to deal with it. The eagerness of the students and the final results will be worth it.

Internet Links:

- *http://sln.fi.edu/tfi/hotlists/energy.html*
  The Franklin Institute has compiled an exhaustive collection of links to "energy" resources.

- *http://www.energy.ca.gov/education*
  You should be able to find the answers to all your questions in the 15 chapters of the "Energy Story." It's great reading and will hold your students' interest.

ROCKS AND SOIL 1

Make a special booklet to show what you've learned about rocks.

Grade Level: three

Duration: about 15 minutes per student on the computer

Materials: a drawing program such as *Kid Pix* or a publishing program such as *The Print Shop*, *PrintMaster Gold*, or *Print Artist*

Procedure: Design and put together a "graduated page" booklet to tell about how the types of rocks are formed.

Before the Computer:

Discuss how igneous rocks are formed from melted minerals, sedimentary rocks are formed when layers of material are pressed together, usually under water, and metamorphic rocks are changed by heat or pressure. Bring examples into the class and let the students examine them. Read about rocks in the textbook or other resource material.

On the Computer:

- Getting the print and the pictures in just the right place on the pages is kind of tricky and may take awhile. For this reason, you should make a template. With your publishing program or your word processor (whatever the children are going to use), draw a line at the place where the fold will be on each paper. You will have several templates for each booklet. This is very time consuming the first time, but then you will have the templates saved and will never need to go through the trauma again. Be sure to change the name before you save the children's pages.

- To find the place to draw the line, place one sheet of paper on top of another (or two or three, depending on how many pages you want). Slide the top sheet one inch (2.54 cm) down from the top of the bottom sheet.

- Fold up the bottom so that all the edges are an equal distance apart. When the pages are printed, they will be stapled on this fold. This is where you need to draw the lines on your templates.

- After the templates are done and labeled page1 front, page1 back, etc., have the children draw their title on the first page and the title of each page on the part of the page that shows when the booklet is closed (see illustration.) If putting the titles on the edges is too difficult, you can print labels and stick them on.

- The information can then be written and illustrated on the pages of the booklet.

ROCKS AND SOIL 1 *(cont.)*

Internet Links:

- *http://walrus.wr.usgs.gov/docs/ask-a-ge.html*
  You and your students can e-mail earth science questions to a geologist at Ask-A-Geologist@usgs.gov. Each message goes to a different USGS earth scientist.

- *http://www.rockhounds.com/rockshop/table.html*
  A large collection of rock and mineral pictures and links can be found here.

- *http://www.arts.ouc.bc.ca/geog/G111/9a.html*
  Peruse an explanation and diagram of the rock cycle.

The Rock Cycle

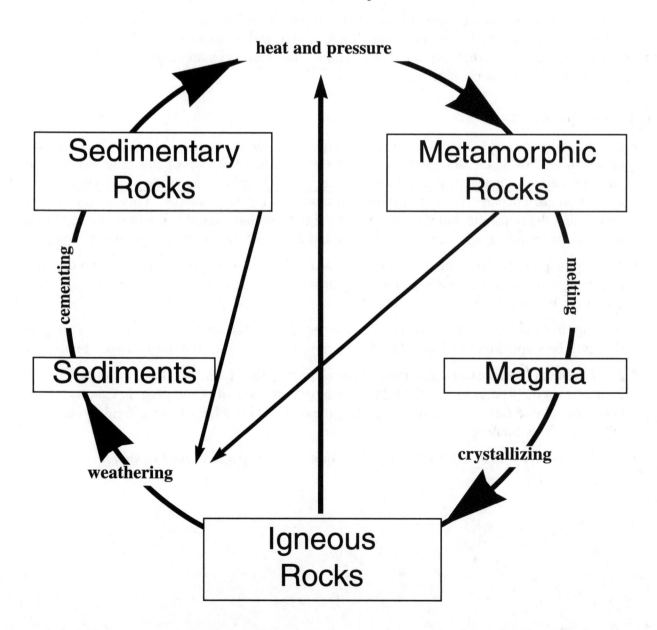

ROCKS AND SOIL 1 *(cont.)*

Minerals melt deep inside the earth. Sometimes melted minerals move to the surface and cool. Then they are called igneous rocks. Granite is an igneous rock. Sometimes the presence of different materials make igneous rocks appear spotted.

ROCKS AND SOIL 2

Learn the importance of keeping records and see how different soils affect plant growth.

Grade Level: three to five

Duration: about 10 minutes a day once a week and then 20–30 minutes to do graphs

Materials: three different types of soil (sand, clay, loam), containers for plants, gravel, bean seedlings (or other easily obtained seedlings), ruler, container for water, drawing program, word processor

Procedure: Grow plants in three different types of soil. Measure and observe to see which plant grows best.

Before the Computer:

- Divide the students into groups.
- Put a half-inch (1.27 cm) of gravel in the bottom of each pot.
- Fill one pot with sand, one with clay, and one with loam (potting soil will do) for each group.
- Label each pot.
- Plant one bean plant in each pot.
- Place the pots where each pot in a group receives the same amount and kind of light.
- Give the plants equal amounts of water at the same intervals and at the same times.
- Measure the plant height and number of leaves per plant weekly for at least six weeks.

On the Computer:

- Record the information on charts you make yourself, using the word processor or a publishing or drawing program.
- Have the students make line or bar graphs to show the results. You can use the charting feature of your spreadsheet if you used one, or a drawing program, or a program such as *The Print Shop* or *Print Artist*.

Internet Links:

- *http://www.rmplc.co.uk/eduweb/sites/allsouls/science/soiltab.html*
  A detailed lesson plan is given for an activity on soil.

- *http://avenue.gen.va.us/Community/Environ/EnvironEdCenter/Habitat/SoilStudy/Sshome.HTML*
  This is a nice site entitled "Soil Study." It has lesson plans, research information, and much more.

ROCKS AND SOIL 2 *(cont.)*

Plant Growth Observations				
Soil Type	**Week**	**Date**	**Plant Height**	**Number of Leaves**
Sand	1			
	2			
	3			
	4			
	5			
	6			
Clay	1			
	2			
	3			
	4			
	5			
	6			
Loam	1			
	2			
	3			
	4			
	5			
	6			

Observations of results and thought questions:

1. Did the plants grow faster in one particular type of soil? What do you think is the reason for this?

   _____

2. Did the plants get more leaves in one particular type of soil? What do you think is the reason for this? _____

   _____

3. Which soil do you think is best for growing bean plants? Why? _____

   _____

4. Compare your results with the other groups in your class. Were they similar? Why do you think this is? _____

   _____

5. What was the most interesting thing about this project?_____

   _____

6. What else can you conclude about the effect of soil on plant growth?_____

   _____

ROCKS AND SOIL 2 *(cont.)*

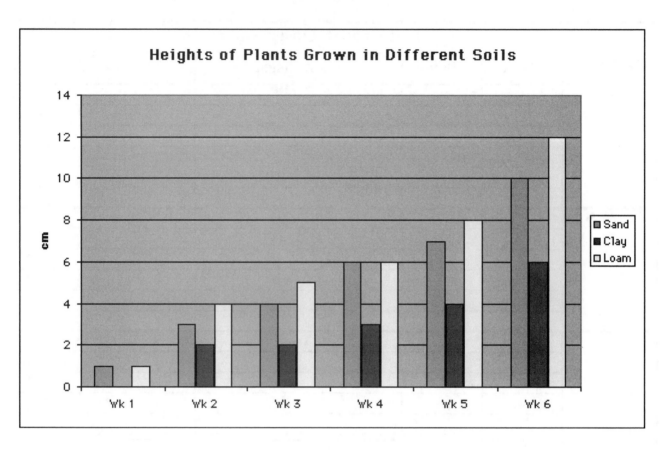

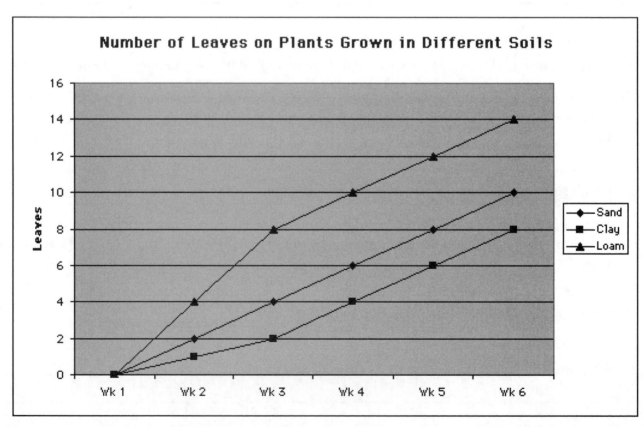

ROCKS AND SOIL 3

Start an Internet project on rocks and minerals.

Grade Level: three to five

Duration: one 30-minute session to set up the project and then about 15 minutes a session, as needed, through the semester for answering letters

Materials: access to e-mail, small rocks and minerals from your local area

Procedure: Trade rock and mineral samples with other children around the world and exchange information, ideas, and culture.

Before the Computer:

- Obtain permission for this project, as postage will cost, and you need to be sure you have money to do this.
- Decide what you are going to trade and what you are going to say in your initial posting.
- As a class, compose the e-mail.
- Research the different rocks and minerals found in your area.
- Collect small rocks and minerals and identify them.
- Package the rocks and minerals to mail.

On the Computer:

- Find a site that has online projects. Several are listed in the "Internet Links" section of this activity.
- Post your project.
- As the responses come in, answer the letters and mail the packages.

Extensions:

- I like to put up a large map and put stickers or pins in it so the students can see where the rocks and minerals originate.
- Make a display of the different rocks and minerals received. Identify and label them.
- Use a digital camera or a regular camera and scanner to photograph your displays and add them to your Web page, if you have one.
- Start an address book of classes you have corresponded with by e-mail. The students will enjoy looking at it and may want to have keypals.

ROCKS AND SOIL 3 *(cont.)*

Internet Links:

- *http://www.gsn.org/project/index.html*
  Not only is there a searchable list of ongoing projects that you might want to join, but here are also archives for past projects that you might want to modify and start again and an opportunity to register your own project so that others might join you.

- *http://www.ziplink.net/users/tlipcon/keypals/*
  Take advantage of the list of teachers and other educators who want to participate in keypal exchanges or online projects or just communicate and exchange ideas.

- *http://www1.minn.net:80/~schubert/EdHelpers.html*
  Here are links to many sites that have projects.

Sample Posting:

- We are in the fifth grade at Hill Country Elementary School in south central Texas. We have a lot of pink granite where we live. Its real name is Town Mountain granite, but everyone around here just calls it "pink granite." It is used for buildings, statues, monuments, and other things. In our area people have also found topaz and diamonds, but we probably will not include a diamond in your sample <smile>. Does your state or country have a particular rock or mineral that is important to your area? It doesn't have to be economically important, just well known. We want to collect rock and mineral samples from all 50 of the United States and from as many other countries around the world as possible. Please send us a small sample from your state or country. E-mail us and tell us all about your sample and all about yourselves. We will send you a sample of our pink granite and other information about Texas. We plan to display our collection of rocks, minerals, and information on our Web page. Please include your e-mail address and the regular mail address for your school or organization so that we can send your sample.

ROCKS AND SOIL 3 *(cont.)*

Rocks and Minerals from Around the World

Type of Rock or Mineral	Where Found	Who Sent It	E-mail Address

CHANGES IN THE EARTH

Make learning vocabulary words fun with word games.

Grade Level: three to five

Duration: 5–15 minutes

Materials: a program that allows you to create word puzzles (There are many of these on the market today. I found more than 50 on the Internet. Most of these are shareware—use a trial version for a while to decide if you want to pay for the full version. Some are commercial packages that you can order or go to your local software outlet to buy.)

Procedure: Create word puzzles to reinforce learning.

Before the Computer:

- Study ways the earth changes. The earth has three layers—the crust, the mantle, and the core.

- Learn about the instruments scientists use to study the earth.

- Learn about weathering and erosion. Discover ways water, plants, and air help weather rocks. Observe how water and wind cause erosion of the soil.

- Explore how earthquakes and volcanoes cause fast changes.

- Develop a list of vocabulary words related to changes in the earth.

On the Computer:

- Using your word puzzle creation software, build puzzles related to the study of changes in the earth.

- Different types of puzzles can be created using the same list of vocabulary words or set of questions and answers. For example, some children who have trouble following lines might do better with a crossword puzzle than they would a word search.

- Some of the puzzle creators allow for a great deal of creativity, such as different shapes for the puzzles, illustrating the puzzles, or using clues instead of just vocabulary words in the word searches.

- These puzzles may be printed on paper for the children to work at their desks or take home, or they can be solved seated at the computer with sound effects and music. Several sites have online word puzzles.

- Most of these programs are user-friendly enough that you may want to allow your students to create puzzles for their classmates to solve.

- Another variation is to use pictures instead of word clues.

CHANGES IN THE EARTH *(cont.)*

Internet Links:

- *http://www.softseek.com/Games/Word/2index.html*
  This is a site that lists many word game sites for you to visit. Some are for playing word games online; some are for word puzzle generators to download.

- *http://www.alberts.com/AuthorPages/00001919/Prod_504.htm*
  Here you can find a word-search puzzle generator that you can download for a trial and then purchase later if you like. The puzzle can be edited in several ways. You can create shaped puzzle grids. The puzzles can be imported into word processors. The only drawback that I could find to this puzzle maker is that it only runs in DOS.

- *http://www.winsite.com/info/pc/win3/games/gtiwrd21.zip/*
  This little shareware program is very interesting. You can play puzzles on screen or print them out to play later. When you play the puzzle on screen, it has sound effects and a 3-D look. It requires vbrun300.dll to run.

- *http://www2.ao.com/~tregan*
  This is an online word search generator.

- *http://www.softseek.com/Games/Word/Review_8357_index.html*
  WordFinder is a word search puzzle maker that allows you to use pictures as hints and also gives crossword style clues instead of single words to search for.

- *http://www.softseek.com/Games/Word/Review_10017_index.html*
  Word Puzzler for Windows lets you create different types of puzzles—crosswords, word searches, vocabulary lists, vocabulary quizzes, and matching puzzles—all from the same word list. It also creates answer keys. Of all the software I reviewed for this activity, I think this one is my favorite.

Changes in the Earth

Write the number of the word's definition next to the word.

	Words		Definitions
_____	lava	1.	large piles of sand forms and moved by the wind
_____	magma	2.	to burst out
_____	erosion	3.	a machine that scientists can use to learn about the earth's crust
_____	seismograph	4.	to wear down or break apart rocks
_____	erupt	5.	hot, melted rock that flows from a volcano
_____	dune	6.	a shaking or sliding of the earth's crust
_____	earthquake	7.	hot, melted rock deep inside the earth

CHANGES IN THE EARTH *(cont.)*

Changes in the Earth

```
Z R C K U E A D B G P W E A E
B G R C P K E E V Y I L M G R
R O P O O A O O J M T Q Y M O
L E T R O U N Q C N L Y M C S
G N S O K H C M K D U D R V O
R B Q E C T L Z P B K S Q K N
E E B R K R O I U M R U T S Y
H G H U S A V S X J Z O W M E
T P Z P D E Y O L M L N G N C
A Z O T C V D E G C
E I C N I D K P H G
W C J A I B D Q K A
G S E I S M O G R A
K W Z X D F M X Y C
```

core   dune   rock

crust   magma   erupt

weather   volcano   erosi

seismograph

Across Clues:

4. When lava cools, it forms ____.

6. hot, melted rock deep inside the earth

7. a machine that scientist can use to learn about the earth's crust

9. to burst out

12. hot, melted rock that flows from a volcano

13. the movement of soil or rocks by wind or water

Down Clues:

1. a shaking or sliding of the earth's crust

2. to wear down or break apart rocks

3. the center part of the earth

5. the outer layer of the earth

8. the middle layer of the earth

10. large piles of sand formed and moved by the wind

11. a mountain with an opening through which lava, ashes, rocks, and other materials come out

CHANGES IN LANDFORMS

One of the ways landforms are changed is by volcanoes. There is much information about volcanoes—in books, in the newspaper, in magazines, on television documentaries, and on the Internet. Once again, a virtual field trip is in order.

Grade Level: five

Duration: probably at least one hour to take the field trip and then additional time for research, if you choose

Materials: access to the Internet (It is nice to have a projection output device or several monitors with a splitter so that the entire class can see easily. If you do not have this, you may want to do this in smaller groups that can gather around your computer screen.)

Procedure: Explore with your students some of the many volcano-related sites on the Internet. You may want to have each child choose some facet of the study of volcanoes to do more research on and make a report to the class. All of the sites in this field trip have intriguing links that just beg to be explored. This would be a great kick-off activity for a longer unit of study.

Note: Any time you are doing this type of activity, it is a good idea to visit all of the sites yourself before going there with the students. Sometimes sites disappear overnight. Sometimes links do not lead exactly where you expect them to. I explored all of the sites listed in this book, but I did not visit all of the links from every one of them.

Before the Computer:

- Explain that landforms are different shapes of land, such as mountains, plains, and plateaus. Discuss some of the ways landforms might change.

On the Computer:

- *http://volcano.und.edu*
  This is a wonderful Web site that you could spend several hours exploring. It is called "Volcano World." At Volcano World you will find the following topics explored at length.

CHANGES IN LANDFORMS *(cont.)*

"Research and Information," which includes information about currently erupting volcanoes, volcanoes of other worlds, and volcanic parks, as well as other items.

"Interact with Us," which has the "Ask a Volcanologist" section, a link you must follow. There are questions and answers on nearly every volcanic subject you can think of. And if your students have a question that is not in the archives, they can ask it and receive the answer by e-mail. This is the section where the students can find subjects for their research if they are having trouble narrowing their topics. Also in this area is the "Eruption Alert." You can register and receive information by e-mail on new eruptions worldwide.

"Volcano Indexes" gives you links to pages about volcanoes around the world. The lists are sorted by world region, country/area, and volcano name.

"Kids' Door" has games, artwork, school activities, and fun for kids.

"Teaching and Learning" has lesson plans for teachers, activities for students, and lots more links.

- *http://vulcan.wr.usgs.gov*
  This is the main page of the Cascades Volcano Observatory. This observatory is located in Washington state and has multiple directions to go in your explorations. You can investigate news and current events dealing with volcanoes, learn the terminology you are likely to encounter in your studies, find out exactly who, what, where, and why about the Cascades Volcano Observatory. There are links to very nice photographs of most of the volcanoes of the world.

- *http://vulcan.wr.usgs.gov/Msh/ljt_slideset_old.html*
  A set of 50 slides of Mount St. Helens includes descriptions and captions.

- *http://vulcan.wr.usgs.gov/Photo/Volcanoes/framework.html*
  See miscellaneous volcano photos with links to information about each of the volcanoes pictured.

- *http://www.dartmouth.edu/~volcano*
  At this site you can find information on active volcanoes all over the world. You can also subscribe to a list server at this site to get updates on volcanic activity and to discuss research. This list server is a little advanced for fifth graders, but the teacher might enjoy it. At this site you can also link to journal articles about active volcanoes. I really enjoyed the maps and pictures.

- *http://www.geo.mtu.edu/volcanoes/world.html*
  Our next stop is a page called "Earth's Active Volcanoes." The page opens with a world map divided into 12 areas. Then under each geographic area is a list of links to volcanoes in that area. It is very useful if you are searching for information on volcanoes in a certain geographic region.

- *http://www.science.uwaterloo.ca/earth/geoscience/hickson.html*
  If your students wonder about who gathers this information and how it is gathered, this stop is for them. It tells all about a career in volcanology. You can find out all of the different jobs that are available in the field and how much and what kind of education you need for each of the jobs.

CHANGES IN LANDFORMS *(cont.)*

- *http://www.libby.org/writingHTML/tut/final.html*
  A lesson on using the Internet to research information on volcanoes can be found at this site, which offers some suggestions about what to include in a research report and a link to information about volcano discoveries on Mars.

- *http://volcano.und.nodak.edu/*
  A great site featuring a listing of major volcano points in the world.

- *http://www.fema.gov/library/volcanof.htm*
  If you stop here, you will find emergency information about volcanoes provided by the Federal Emergency Management Agency. This site includes some very interesting facts about volcanoes, and some suggestions about how to raise community awareness in areas of volcanic activity.

- *http://www.geo.mtu.edu/volcanoes/hazards.html*
  In the introduction to her page, Colleen M. Riley states, "Volcanoes are beneficial to humans living on or near them. They produce fertile soil and provide valuable minerals, water reservoirs, geothermal resources, and scenic beauty. But volcanoes can be very dangerous. Where can a person go to be safe from an erupting volcano? What types of volcanic hazards might they face? These questions are difficult to answer because there are many types of volcanic eruptions which produce different types of volcanic hazards." She then gives links to examples of different types of eruptions and summaries of what can be found at each link—a very interesting page. I hadn't realized the vast differences in eruptions.

- *http://vulcan.wr.usgs.gov/home.html*
  At this site, you will find an alphabetical list of volcanoes from around the world, photo archives, a virtual visit through the Cascade Volcanoes, information on how to live with volcanoes, and more! News updates on current volcanic activity as well as links to other volcano sites are included.

- *http://www.cotf.edu/ete/moved/scen/volcanoes/volcanoes.html*
  This is the final stop on today's field trip. This is a very nicely organized site that is perfect for research. It has a vast amount of information, all arranged in outline form. Some of the things you can investigate here are

  "Volcanology: Volcanoes as individuals." This includes links to pages on types of volcanoes (some very nice drawings here), types of lava, sizes of eruptions, and volcano eruption animations.

  "Volcanoes and the Earth: Volcanoes as a group." Links here are to locations of volcanoes, plate tectonics, and looking inside the earth.

  "Living with Volcanoes." Pages under this heading are volcanoes and climate, monitoring volcanoes, volcanic hazards, and dealing with volcanic threats.

I hope you and your students enjoyed our little trip and bookmarked some places to return to when you have more time.

OCEANS

There are about 100 species of mammals that depend on fresh water or the ocean for part or all of their lives. After studying about some of these mammals, the students can express their learning by designing and writing a booklet.

Grade Level: three to five

Duration: one class period

Materials: a word processing program or a publishing program such as *Microsoft Publisher*, *The Print Shop Press Writer*, or *Student Writing Center*

Procedure: Create a marine mammal book after studying about mammals that live in the sea.

Before the Computer:

- Learn that marine mammals are mammals that have adapted to life in the ocean. They have all the characteristics of mammals—breathing air through lungs, bearing live young, producing milk, having hair or fur, and being warm-blooded—yet look very different and live very differently from most other mammals.

- Learn the basic groups of marine mammals:

    Pinnipeds are "flipper-footed." This group includes true seals, fur seals, sea lions, and walruses.

    Cetaceans include whales, dolphins, and porpoises.

    Sirenians are plant-eating mammals that live where the water is warm. This group includes manatees and dugongs.

    Sea otters are the smallest marine mammals.

    Some scientists include polar bears as marine mammals because they spend so much time in the water, can swim very long distances, and get most of their food from the ocean.

On the Computer:

- Set up the page on your word processor so that it will print on a half page. This will need to be set to landscape orientation and book fold (in *Publisher*) or Booklet (in *Press Writer*)

- Have the students write

    a narrative of what they have learned about sea mammals,

    a report on their favorite sea mammal,

    an original story about their favorite sea mammal,

    a poem (or several poems), or

    any other writing that will express what they have learned.

- Encourage the students to decorate the covers of their books and illustrate their writing using a drawing program, a scanned drawing or picture, a hand-drawn illustration, or any other illustration.

OCEANS *(cont.)*

- It makes a nicer book if you use cardstock for the covers. This is heavy bond paper and can be purchased at an office supply or educational supply store.

Internet Links:

- *http://seawifs.gsfc.nasa.gov:80/OCEAN_PLANET/HTML/oceanography_plan.html*
  The Ocean Planet Exhibit at the Smithsonian is featured at this site.

- *http://www.rain.org/~inverts/WHALECORP/cetacea1.htm*
  Discover facts about cetaceans.

- *http://www.redshift.com/~estarr/acs/*
  Here are some photos and information about marine mammals.

- *http://www.seaworld.org/bottlenose_dolphin/bottlenose_dolphins.html*
  Sea World's information on bottlenosed dolphins is at this stie.

- *http://www.seaotters.org/*
  This excellent page by the Friends of the Sea Otter contains some fun "kid stuff."

- *http://www.seaworld.org/* (click on Animal Resources for a great list of dolphin and marine mammal information)
  There are lots of dolphin and other marine mammal pictures here. The page takes a long time to load.

- *http://badger.ac.brocku.ca/~sg94ae/*
  This is "Sheila's Marine Mammal Page." She has many marine mammal links and some good information, as well as some good pictures.

- *http://www.whaletimes.org/whafshn.htm*
  "Fishing for Facts on the Whale Times" site is a great place for students to learn about marine mammals.

EARTH'S CHANGING CRUST

Tracking the world's earthquakes and making predictions based on data gathered gives the students a better understanding of the movement of the earth's plates and the results of that movement.

Grade Level: five

Duration: about 10 minutes a day for three weeks

Materials: line maps of the world with longitude and latitude, maps showing the location of the world's tectonic plates, access to the Internet, colored pencils, pens, or markers

Procedure: Chart the world's earthquakes on a map and observe how earthquakes are related to the earth's plates.

Before the Computer:

- Discuss the current theory, that the earth's surface is made up of many large slabs of rock, called plates, which "float" on the semi-fluid rock below.

- Discuss that the continents have moved and that the plate boundaries have also changed.

- Talk about how the earth's lithosphere has been split up and put back together many times, leaving scars called faults.

- Guide the students to understand that most earthquakes happen when the pressure builds up under these plates, causing a fault to rupture.

- Learn that scientists who study earthquakes are called seismologists.

- Discuss seismographs and other measuring and mapping tools.

- Ask the students to form a hypothesis about how earthquakes are predicted.

On the Computer:

- Go to *http://civeng.carleton.ca/cgi-bin2/quakes* on the Internet for a list of recent earthquakes. Try *http://quake.wr.usgs.gov* if the above site is busy. The headings at the top of the chart stand for Date, Time, Latitude, Longitude, Depth (in kilometers), Magnitude (with the method used to calculate it), and Location Quality (A is good; D is bad).

- Divide the students into groups. Give each group line maps and a tectonic plate map.

- On the line map for each group, have the students locate each earthquake, using latitude and longitude.

- Put a mark for each earthquake. Use a different color for each whole number representing magnitude (red for 2.0–2.99, green for 3.0–3.99, purple for 4.0–4.99, etc.).

- Continue this activity for two weeks.

- If the students have not already seen one, suggest that there might be a pattern developing.

EARTH'S CHANGING CRUST *(cont.)*

- Compare the line map with the plate tectonic map.

- Using this information, have the students predict where an earthquake will occur the next week.

- On a clean line map, draw a circle around the area (small) of the prediction. Chart the earthquakes for another week to check the accuracy of the predictions.

Internet Links:

- *http://vflylab.calstatela.edu/edesktop/VirtApps/VirtualEarthQuake/VQuakeIntro.html*
  If the students measure carefully and accurately and work all the way through the virtual earthquake project, they will get a certificate.

- *http://www.ceri.memphis.edu/www/public_info/follies.html*
  Facts and follies about earthquakes can be found here.

- *http://www.geophys.washington.edu/seismosurfing.html*
  An extensive list of links to earthquake information is located here.

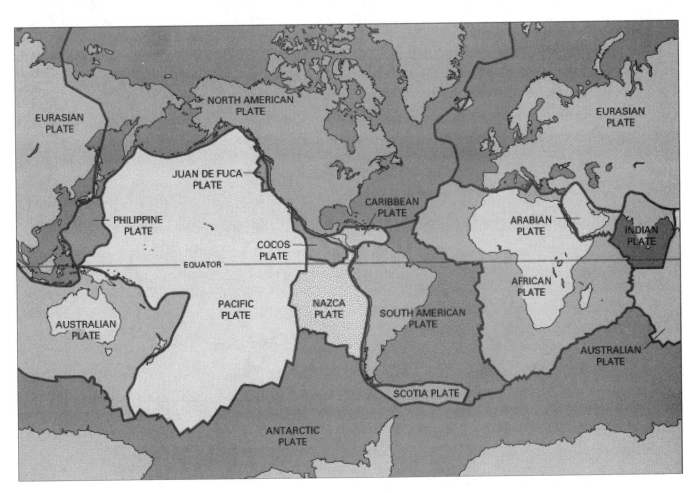

EARTH'S CHANGING CRUST (cont.)

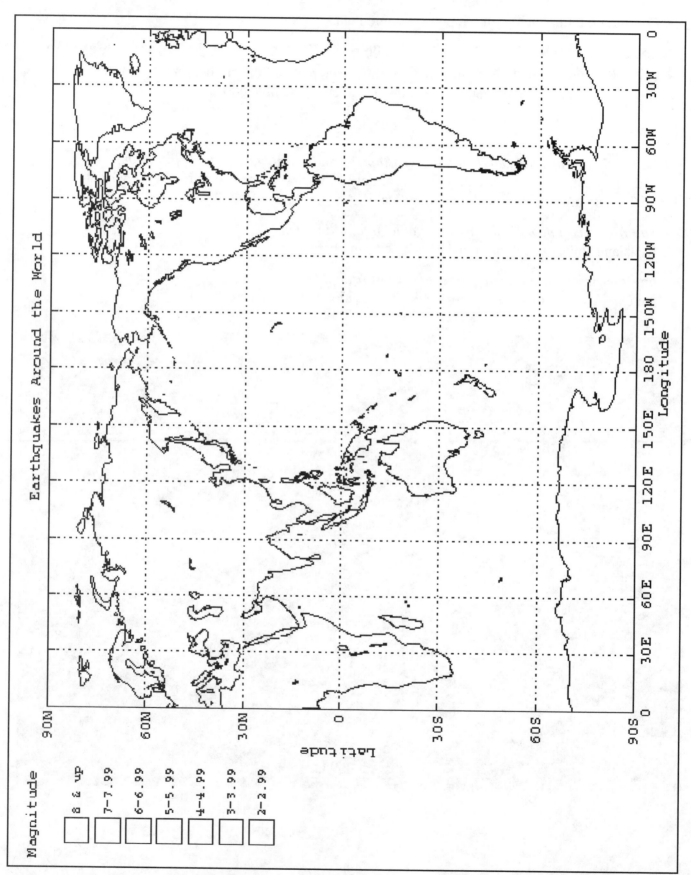

PROTECTING THE ENVIRONMENT

Portray your sentiments about protecting the environment and learn creative ways to use your word processor or desktop publishing program at the same time.

Grade Level: three to five

Duration: 10 minutes

Materials: a desktop publishing program such as *The Print Shop*, *Printmaster Gold*, *Print Artist*, etc.; clear laminating film (contact paper, for example)

Procedure: Make bumper stickers for the children to display on their parents' cars, their bicycles, or elsewhere.

Before the Computer:

- Discuss slogans and plan designs for bumper stickers.

On the Computer:

- Using the desktop publishing program, design colorful and creative bumper stickers with environmental slogans that the children make up.

- Use the landscape page setup and put a border around an area about three inches (eight cm) tall.

- After the bumper stickers are printed and cut out, cut a rectangle of contact paper slightly larger than the bumper sticker.

- Carefully peel the backing off and place the bumper sticker facedown in the center of the contact paper.

- Replace the backing. It can be removed again just before the sticker is applied.

Internet Links:

- *http://www.globe.gov*
  "Global Learning and Observations to Benefit the Environment" (GLOBE) is a worldwide network of students, teachers, and scientists working together to study and understand the global environment. GLOBE students make a core set of environmental observations at or near their schools and report their data via the Internet. Scientists use GLOBE data in their research and provide feedback to the students to enrich their science education.

- *http://wcmc.org.uk/cis/*
  The World Conservation Monitoring Centre (WCMC) provides information services on conservation and sustainable use of the world's living resources. Their collection of databases include species, protected areas, forests, marine life, and national biodiversity files.

PROTECTING THE ENVIRONMENT *(cont.)*

Help Save Our Lakes — Xeriscape!

Get the Lead Out! Keep the Emission Controls on Your Car

Breathe Free — Stop Air Pollution

CLOUDS AND STORMS

Learn the different types of clouds and in what weather conditions they are present.

Grade Level: three to five

Duration: two weeks for observations and one class period for reports and bulletin board creation.

Materials: observation and research sheets, encyclopedias (electronic or paper), access to the Internet (optional)

Procedure: Create a bulletin board using illustrated reports.

Before the Computer:

- Research the types of clouds:

    Cirrus Clouds—Cirrus means "curl." Cirrus clouds are made of ice crystals in a high cold atmosphere. They are often seen in good weather.

    Cumulus Clouds—Cumulus means "heap." Cumulus clouds are white, puffy, fair-weather clouds. They are usually closer to the ground than cirrus clouds.

    Cumulonimbus Clouds—Nimbus means "rain." Cumulonimbus clouds are huge cumulus clouds that look like anvils or towers in the sky. They usually signal stormy weather. Lightning, thunder, and high winds are usually found in cumulonimbus clouds.

    Stratus—Stratus means "stretched out." Stratus clouds are gray clouds that are very low to the ground. Stratus clouds are formed in sheets or layers and spread out over the sky, often blocking out the sun. Oftentimes stratus clouds are present during rain.

- Observe the sky for two weeks and identify the types of clouds seen. Have the students write in their journals what types of clouds they observe and what the weather is like at the time.

On the Computer:

- Search the Internet for information and pictures or use encyclopedias for the research.

- Capture the pictures from the Internet or draw pictures of the different types of clouds.

- Have the students write a report about what they have learned, illustrating it with their pictures.

- Place the reports on the bulletin board to share with other classes.

Internet Links:

- *http://www.nssl.noaa.gov*
  Thunderstorm resources are listed here.

- *http://ww2010.atmos.uiuc.edu/(Gh)/guides/mtr/cld/home.rxml*
  This is a fantastic cloud page.

- *http://www.public.iastate.edu/~intruder/weather/weather.htm*
  Weather World has video clips of thunderstorms.

- *http://australiansevereweather.simplenet.com/photography/index.html*
  Many, many photographs from Australia categorized into cloud types can be found here.

CLOUDS AND STORMS *(cont.)*

Cloud and Weather Observation Chart			
Date	**Time**	**Types of Clouds**	**Weather**

MEASURING WEATHER CONDITIONS

Compare weather in different parts of the country and chart the results.

Grade Level: three to five

Duration: one week for research, 15 minutes a day; one class period for compiling data and building classroom charts

Materials: access to the Internet, newspaper with nationwide weather, and/or the Weather Channel

Procedure: Chart and compare the weather in different parts of the country. During the week, discuss why different parts of the country have different types of weather. Discuss how the Great Lakes affect the weather in that part of the country. Have the students think about how the coastal cities compare with the inland cities at about the same latitude. Is the weather noticeably different on the East Coast than it is on the West Coast? Is the weather the same on both sides of the Rocky Mountains? What affects it? The students can think of many more discussion topics than I can write here.

Before the Computer:

- Have each student choose four different cities in various parts of the country.
- Locate the cities on the individual maps, mark them, and enter their names on the chart.

On the Computer:

- Chart the weather (temperature and precipitation) every day for one week.
- Use the Weather Channel to receive reports for your cities.
- Some newspapers and magazines have nationwide weather reports.
- The Internet sites in the "Internet Links" section of this activity have weather reports.

Student Directions:

- After charting the temperature and precipitation for five days,

    find the average temperature for the four cities.

    record the high temperature for the four cities.

    record the low temperature for the four cities.

- Compare the charts of all the students in the class.

    Find the average temperature for the entire class.

    Find the highest temperature for the entire class.

    Find the lowest temperature for the entire class.

    Discover which areas of the country have the most and least precipitation.

- Put flags on your classroom map for each category above.

MEASURING WEATHER CONDITIONS *(cont.)*

Internet Links:

- *http://www.weather.com/twc/homepage.twc*
  The Weather Channel gives five-day forecasts, current conditions, temperatures, barometric pressure, and wind velocity.

- *http://usatoday.com/weather/wfront.htm*
  This site includes forecasts but no current conditions. However, there are many interesting links, including one that has teacher activities and projects.

- *http://cirrus.sprl.umich.edu/wxnet/*
  This is a very comprehensive weather site with many links.

- *http://groundhog.sprl.umich.edu/*
  This is a link from the Weathernet, but I thought it deserved special mention. It has weather for any zip code in the U.S.A., K–12 lesson plans for teaching weather, and collaborative projects such as "One Sky Many Voices."

- *http://covis.atmos.uiuc.edu/covis/visualizer*
  General weather information and resources can be found here.

- *http://www.itl.net/Education/online/weather/measureind.html*
  Here is an excellent site on measuring precipitation, sunshine, wind velocity and direction, temperature, humidity, cloud cover, atmospheric pressure, and visibility.

- *http://nesen.unl.edu/activities/weather/caffey/caffey.html*
  This weather unit was perpared by a pre-service science teacher.

MEASURING WEATHER CONDITIONS *(cont.)*

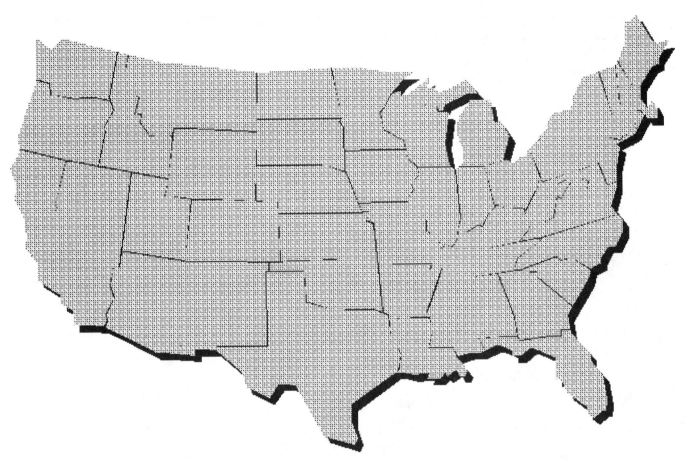

Temperature and Precipitation Chart

City	Day 1		Day 2		Day 3		Day 4		Day 5		Average	
	T	P	T	P	T	P	T	P	T	P	T	P

CLIMATE

Learn how the climate is different in different parts of the world, how different things affect climate, and how the climate affects people's ways of life.

Grade Level: four to five

Duration: two class periods

Materials: encyclopedias (electronic and hard copy), Internet, atlas, *World Almanac*, library books, word processing program

Procedure: Research and learn how climate is determined by the shape of the earth, the tilt of the earth, location on the earth, and many other things.

Before the Computer:

• Have the students choose a place they would like to have an interesting vacation.

• Discuss

> how the tilt of the earth and the shape of the earth determine how much sunshine a location receives.
>
> how climate is different from weather.
>
> how land and water affect temperature.
>
> how ocean currents affect climates.
>
> how elevation affects climate.
>
> how mountains affect precipitation.

On the Computer (and other resources):

• Have each student research his or her chosen vacation spot and write a narrative about "My Vacation." Include information about what kind of climate the area has, how the people live, what kinds of clothes they wear, etc.

Internet Links:

• *http://www.wrcc.sage.dri.edu/rcc.html*
U.S. Regional Climate Centers are listed here.

• *http://drylands.nasm.edu:1995/panel2.html*
Here you can find information about arid and semi-arid lands.

• *http://www.aws.com/globalwx.html*
Click to find information about many places.

• *http://www.aws.com/vschool/index.html*
I hope this site is active by the time this book is published. It is supposed to be an extensive weather and climate site full of different activities, including a teacher chat room to talk about how you are teaching about weather and climate.

SUN, MOON, AND PLANETS

"Let's pretend" is a fun activity for all ages, and everyone likes to think about visiting faraway places. So combine the two and create your own Interplanetary Travel Agency.

Grade Level: three to five

Duration: several days for research, two class periods for design and printing

Materials: encyclopedias (both electronic and hard copy), access to the Internet, library books, a publishing program such as *Microsoft Publisher* or Brøderbund's *Press Writer*

Procedure: Have the students design and print advertising copy for their travel agency. Some will do brochures, some posters, some flyers, and some letters for a mailing. Each must include actual information about the chosen vacation spot and reasons why someone would want to visit. This, of course, must be fictional, but the students will need to base it on information they have about the planet, moon, etc.

Before the Computer:

- Discuss the ways travel agencies advertise—brochures, posters, letters, discounts, newspaper ads, etc.

- Have students research the solar system in general and decide which planet, asteroid, moon, etc., they will develop as a tourist attraction.

- Each student will do research on his or her choice and use the information to design the advertising material.

On the Computer:

- Have the students use a publishing program such as *Press Writer*, *Publisher*, *Printmaster Gold*, or *The Print Shop* to design, create, and print advertising material for their agency.

- You may want to design and print a research sheet to aid in the research or reproduce the one on the next page.

Internet Links:

There is so much wonderful information on the Internet about the solar system that the mind just boggles with the very difficult task of narrowing it down to what you can spare time to visit.

- *http://seds.lpl.arizona.edu/billa/tnp/overview.html*
  An overview of the solar system, this site has everything your students will need for their study of the solar system—very extensive with nice pictures and links.

- *http://seds.lpl.arizona.edu/nineplanets/nineplanets/nineplanets.html*
  This multimedia trip through the solar system has pages not only for the sun and the planets but also for each moon of each planet and much, much more.

- *http://ranier.oact.hq.nasa.gov/Sensors_page/Planets.html*
  There is so much information and so many links that you could spend several days right here!

SUN, MOON, AND PLANETS *(cont.)*

- *http://www.eduplace.com/rdg/gen_act/advent/solar.html*
  This lesson plan for writing science fiction is based on solar system research.

- *http://chico.rice.edu//armadillo/Simulations/Mars_Project/mars.html*
  This Internet project is a simulation of a trip to Mars.

- *http://www-hpcc.astro.washington.edu/scied/astro/astroindex.html*
  The history of astronomy can be found here, as well as many wonderful images, online courses, lesson plans, and more.

- *http://www.beakman.com/*
  "You Can" is a great site with links to lots of space pictures and photographs from the Hubble telescope. Be sure to click on the can when you first arrive. It's an activity that the students love.

- *http://heasarc.gsfc.nasa.gov/docs/StarChild/*
  "StarChild" is a learning center for young astronomers.

- *http://quest.arc.nasa.gov/mars/*
  The "Live From Mars" site even has a live videocam and a chat room so that your students can discuss what they have learned about Mars.

- *http://www.jpl.nasa.gov/mpfmir/*
  You can find links to learn all about Mars Pathfinder, Mars Global Surveyor, and Mars Surveyor '98.

SUN, MOON, AND PLANETS *(cont.)*

Name:	**Subject of research:**
Distance from Earth	
Distance from Sun	
Atmosphere	
Gravity	
Temperature	
What you will pass on the way	
Size	
Length of day	
Length of year	
Discoverer	
Weather	
Surface features	
Number of satellites (moons)	
Rings?	

Other Interesting Facts

SUN, MOON, AND PLANETS (cont.)

Before returning home, be sure to drop by the Hubble Telescope for your souvenir pictures of Saturn and its rings.

For the Vacation of Your Life..... Choose

Saturn

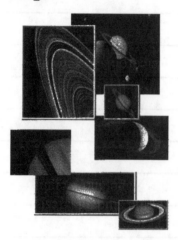

Plan day trips on Voyager to any of Saturn's more than 18 Satellites

Tri-fold Brochure-front and back

Windsurf at Saturn's equator, where you'll whiz along at up to 1,100 miles per hour!

Spend Christmas on Saturn's Ring System. Some of the amusements include throwing snowballs and exploring icebergs.

You only have to step outside your pressure chamber to fill your balloons because along with Hydrogen, Saturn's atmosphere contains helium.

Your vacation will leave you with memories as golden as Saturn's color.

MOVEMENT IN THE SOLAR SYSTEM 1

Finding out how much you would weigh and what your age would be on other planets is fascinating.

Grade Level: three to five

Duration: one class period

Materials: a spreadsheet and a gravitational pull and revolution chart

Procedure: Design a spreadsheet that will, depending on the skill of the students, test their ability to calculate their weight and age on various planets, or just tell them their age and weight.

Before the Computer:

- Discuss

    the fact that each planet moves around the sun in a path called an orbit.

    that all the objects in the solar system—planets, moons, meteoroids, asteroids, and comets—are tied to the sun by its gravity.

    that each planet has different amounts of gravitational pull.

    that the gravitational pull of a planet determines how much we "weigh."

    that to find what you would weigh on another planet you can multiply your weight on Earth by the gravitation factor for that planet.

    that we calculate a "year" as one revolution around the sun.

    that different planets take different amounts of time to revolve around the sun, and why.

    that to find your age according to the length of another planet's year, you would divide your age in Earth years by the period of revolution of that planet.

On the Computer:

- Open the spreadsheet program.

- Learn how to use cells and formulas in a spreadsheet.

- Design the spreadsheet so that it has a cell to enter Earth age and one to enter Earth weight.

- List the planets, the gravitational pull, and the period of revolution in separate columns.

- In another column, enter formulas to calculate age.

- In another column, enter formulas to calculate weight.

- If your students are skilled in multiplication and division, it is fun to use if/else statements to allow the students to test their skills.

MOVEMENT IN THE SOLAR SYSTEM 1 *(cont.)*

Internet Links:

- *http://www.athena.ivv.nasa.gov/curric/space/planets/planorbi.html*
  This is an article about orbits and properties of the planets.

- *http://heasarc.gsfc.nasa.gov/docs/StarChild/*
  Excellent site for the young astronomer.

- *http://www.seti-inst.edu/sci-det.html*
  "Cosmic Wheels—Measuring the Orbits of the Planets" is an activity that you do outside. They
  want you to have one of their videotapes to watch, but most of it you can figure out for yourself.

- *http://oposite.stsci.edu/pubinfo/education/amazing-space*
  As you have probably noticed, the more colorful and graphic a site is, the better I like it. This one
  is impressive! There is a section about collecting trading cards. The way you collect a card is by
  answering questions about certain space objects. There is an area that is still under construction
  that will trace a star through birth, life, death, and rebirth. Hopefully, it will be working by the
  time this book is out. This site is really a must see.

- *http://www.seds.org/galaxy/*
  The Galaxy Page is another outstanding site. There are pages here on each planet, the sun,
  comets, asteroids, other solar systems, astronomy, visions of the future, aerospace, astronautics,
  and much more.

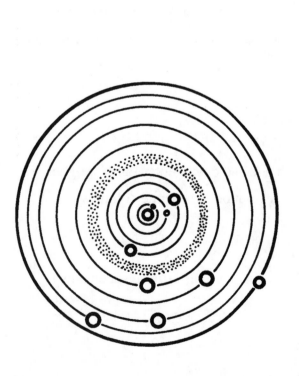

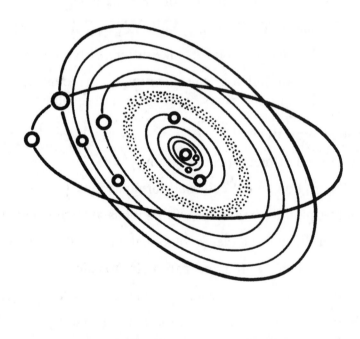

MOVEMENT IN THE SOLAR SYSTEM 1 *(cont.)*

Planet Gravitational Pull and Revolution Chart

Planet	Gravitational Pull	Time for One Revolution
Mercury	0.38 of Earth's	87.9 Earth days
Venus	0.91 of Earth's	224.7 Earth days
Mars	0.38 of Earth's	686.9 Earth days
Jupiter	2.54 of Earth's	11.86 Earth years
Saturn	0.93 of Earth's	29.46 Earth years
Uranus	0.8 of Earth's	84.01 Earth years
Neptune	1.2 of Earth's	164.79 Earth years
Pluto	0.04 of Earth's	248 Earth years

MOVEMENT IN THE SOLAR SYSTEM 1 *(cont.)*

Examples of Spreadsheets

Age and Weight on Different Planets

	A	B	C	D	E	F	G
1							
2							
3	Enter your weight here:		87				
4	Enter your age here:		10				
5							
6	Planet	Gravity	Length of year		Your Age	Your Weight	
7		compared to Earth	in Earth days		in Earth years		
8							
9	Mercury	0.38	87.90		2.41	33.06	
10	Venus	0.91	224.70		6.15	79.17	
11	Earth	1.00	365.24		10.00	87.00	
12	Mars	0.38	686.90		18.81	33.06	
13	Jupiter	2.54	4331.75		118.60	220.98	
14	Saturn	0.93	10759.97		294.60	80.91	
15	Uranus	0.80	30683.81		840.10	69.60	
16	Neptune	1.20	60187.90		1647.90	104.40	
17	Pluto	0.04	88347.52		2418.89	3.48	
18							
19							

Age and Weight on Different Planets

	A	B	C	D	E	F
1						
2						
3	Enter your weight here:		87			
4	Enter your age here:		10			
5						
6	Planet	Gravity	Length of year		Your Age	Your Weight
7		compared to Earth	in Earth days		in Earth years	
8						
9	Mercury	0.38	87.9		=C9*$C4/365.24	=B9*C3
10	Venus	0.91	224.7		=C10*$C4/365.24	=B10*C3
11	Earth	1	365.24		=C11*$C4/365.24	=B11*C3
12	Mars	0.38	686.9		=C12*$C4/365.24	=B12*C3
13	Jupiter	2.54	=11.86*365.24		=C13*$C4/365.24	=B13*C3
14	Saturn	0.93	=29.46*365.24		=C14*$C4/365.24	=B14*C3
15	Uranus	0.8	=84.01*365.24		=C15*$C4/365.24	=B15*C3
16	Neptune	1.2	=164.79*365.24		=C16*$C4/365.24	=B16*C3
17	Pluto	0.04	=248*356.24		=C17*$C4/365.24	=B17*C3
18						
19						

MOVEMENT IN THE SOLAR SYSTEM 2

Eavesdrop on the astronauts and the Shuttle crew.

Grade Level: three to five

Duration: varies

Materials: access to the Internet and *RealAudio* (can be downloaded)

Procedure: You and your class can listen to NASA Television audio of Space Shuttle missions and view the Shuttle and crew.

Before the Computer:

- Discuss any current missions.

- *http://www.nasa.gov*
  You can find information on current NASA activities at the NASA Web site.

On the Computer:

- Go to *http://www.nasa.gov* (click on NTV)
  You can then go to NASA TV for slow-scan pictures of the mission. Choose *RealAudio Live* for the audio broadcast of the shuttle missions. You can view the video using the *CU-SeeMe* program from Cornell University.

Internet Links:

- *http://www.nasa.gov/gallery/*
  Visit the Photo Gallery, Audio Gallery, and Video Gallery at NASA in case you missed something.

- *http://www.cuseeme.com*
  You can download a trial version of *CU-SeeMe* here.

MAPPING THE STARS 1

Using a spreadsheet program, create a star map.

Grade Level: four to five

Duration: one class period

Materials: a spreadsheet program, a star map

Procedure: Using coordinates and a spreadsheet, the students will locate the different stars in several constellations and mark them.

Before the Computer:

- Change the widths of the columns in your spreadsheet so that the cells are square.
- Print out the spreadsheet, making sure that you print the gridlines.
- Shrink or enlarge the star map as needed.
- Lay the star map over the printed spreadsheet and mark with a pin or sharp pencil where the stars in each constellation are.
- Make a list of the coordinates for the stars in each constellation.
- With the students, discuss the following topics

    mapping techniques.

    finding locations on a grid by using X,Y coordinates

    how much like a map grid the spreadsheet is

On the Computer:

- Open the spreadsheet program.
- Give the students the coordinates of the stars in the constellations.
- Use a different letter to designate each constellation.
- Mark the stars in each constellation on the spreadsheet.
- Print out the "constellation map."

Examples: The coordinates I used in the example are

- Cassiopeia: (Q, 1) (W, 2) (P, 4) (T, 4) (X, 5)
- Cepheus: (L, 6) (O, 8) (J, 10) (T, 11) (N, 12)
- Draco: (H, 22) (L, 22) (G, 24) (K, 24) (W, 27) (Z, 27) (L, 28) (H, 30) (L, 30), (S, 30) (N, 31) (J, 32) (G, 33) (I, 34)
- Hercules: (D, 9) (B, 12) (E, 12) (E, 14) (C, 15) (G, 16) (E, 18) (I, 19) (E, 20) (D, 22)(E, 22)
- Ursa Minor: (X, 17) (T, 18) (T, 20) (P, 22) (R, 22) (Q, 25) (S, 25)
- Ursa Major: (AC, 30) (AE, 32) (Z, 33) (V, 34) (W, 34) (AB, 35) (R, 37)

MAPPING THE STARS 1 *(cont.)*

Internet Links:

- *http://spacelink.nasa.gov/index.html*
  This is one of the NASA sites telling about space exploration.

- *http://www.astro.wisc.edu/~dolan/constellations/constellations.html*
  "The Constellations and Their Stars"—This page has much information about the night sky, such as links to alphabetical lists of stars, alphabetical lists of constellations, and interactive sky charts.

- *http://www.cnde.iastate.edu/staff/jtroeger/astronomy.html*
  This online astronomy course could be easily adapted to the fourth or fifth grade level.

- *http://www.aspsky.org/*
  This is the site for the Astronomical Society of the Pacific. One of the neatest things on this site is their free teacher newsletter, "Universe in the Classroom." You can read it online or subscribe to the paper version.

- *http://www.atm.dal.ca/~andromed/*
  I have never seen so many links in one place!

- *http://earthspace.net/~kmiles.dln/9-95/cultures.html*
  Read the myths surrounding the constellations.

- *http://earthspace.net/~kmiles/index3.html*
  There are many more stories and articles about the myths surrounding the constellations at the Astronomy and Earth Science.

- *http://www.pa.msu.edu:80/abrams/*
  Abrams Planetarium at Michigan State University has star maps, information about planetariums, and images.

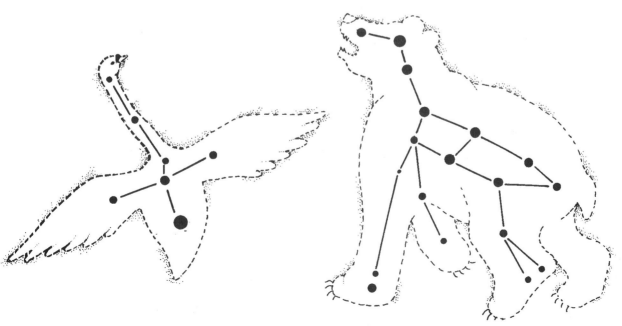

MAPPING THE STARS 1 (cont.)

	A	B	C	D	E	F	G	H	I	J	K	L	M	N	O	P	Q	R	S	T	U	V	W	X	Y	Z	AA	AB	AC	AD	AE
1																	W														
2																							W								
3																															
4													W			W															
5																						W									
6							C																								
7																															
8													C																		
9				H																											
10											C								C												
11																															
12		H			H							C																			
13																															
14					H																										
15			H																												
16							H																								
17																						O									
18					H														O												
19								H																							
20					H													O													
21																															
22			H	H		D				D					O		O														
23																															
24						D			D																						
25															O		O														
26																															
27																						D		D							
28								D																							
29																															
30						D			D					D															X		
31											D																				
32							D																								X
33					D																				X						
34						D													X	X											
35																										X					
36																															
37																	X														

W=Cassiopeia

C=Cepheus

D=Draco

H=Hercules

X=Ursa Major

O=Ursa Minor

MAPPING THE STARS 2

Explore the mythology connected with the constellations.

Grade Level: three to five

Duration: two class periods

Materials: encyclopedias, library books, access to the Internet, a word processing program

Procedure: After mapping the constellations, research and report on the various myths connected with them.

Before the Computer:

- Research in encyclopedias and other reference books to find out about the myths.

On the Computer:

- Research on the Internet to find myths.

- When your research is done, write a report to go with your star map.

Internet Links:

- *http://www.modcult.brown.edu/students/angell/mythology.html*
  Learn about twins in astrology.

- *http://ncnatural.com/NCNatural/stars/sumrstar.html*
  Constellations in the summer sky and their stories can be found here.

- *http://www.iac.es/galeria/slouren/const_node0.html*
  Iroquois and Tewa myths as well as classical mythology are on this site.

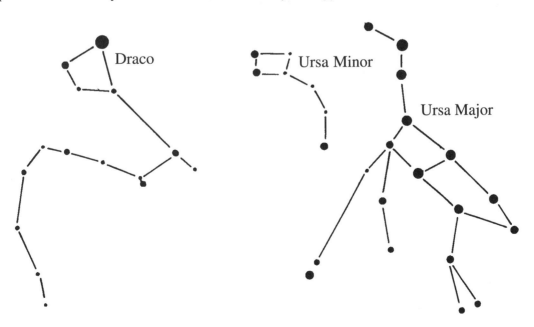

Draco

Ursa Minor

Ursa Major

THE BODY'S SUPPORT

An interactive drill/quiz is fun to make and fun to use.

Grade Level: five

Duration: If the students are familiar with the presentation program, they should be able to make the quiz in two class periods. After it is finished, it shouldn't take more than 10 minutes per student to go through it, though most will want to go through it several times.

Materials: a presentation program such as *HyperStudio*, the names of the bones in the skeleton

Procedure: Make a program that will show the skeleton, and quiz the user on the names of the bones.

Before the Computer:

- Get a picture of a skeleton. You may want to draw one, scan one, or find one in readymade clip art programs. Mine came from *Task Force Clip Art*, by New Vision Technologies.

On the Computer:

- Using a presentation program such as *HyperStudio*, make buttons on each bone.
- Give a name of a bone in a text box, and the user will click on the button for the bone.
- Have messages for both correct and incorrect answers. (My students gave hints as the response to a wrong answer, but that is much more involved than just one stock answer for all incorrect answers and takes a great deal more time.)
- Save the program for future use.

Internet Links:

- *http://calvertnet.k12.md.us/instruction/lessons/skeletons/skeleton.html*
  Activities here are from an elementary school in Maryland.

- *http://www.anatomical.com/chartsfullsize/skeletal.html*
  Here is a very nice image of a skeleton that you might want to use.

- *http://science.coe.uwf.edu/sh/curr/skeletal/skeleton.htm*
  This page was done by an elementary student in Florida.

THE BODY'S SUPPORT *(cont.)*

HyperStudio card

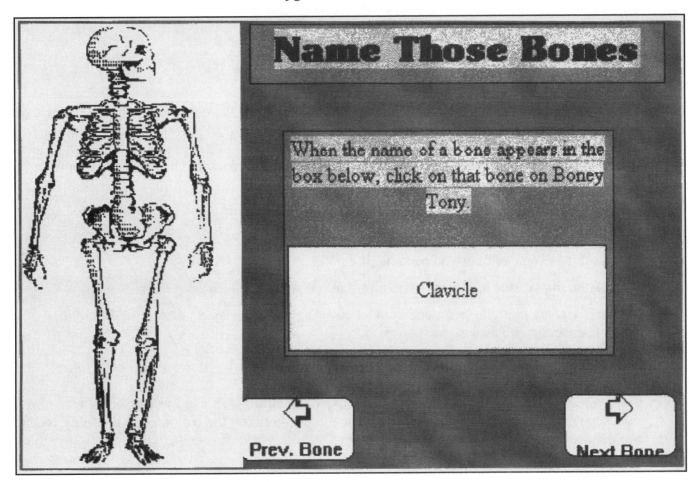

YOUR BODY'S HEALTH NEEDS

Learn about nutrition, exercise, first aid, etc., while creating a useful booklet to take home for family use.

Grade Level: three to five

Duration: one week

Materials: a program such as *Microsoft Publisher*, *Press Writer*, or *Student Writing Center* or any word processor

Procedure: After discussing health needs with the class, make a booklet that has health tips in it.

Before the Computer:

- Discuss ways you can keep your body healthy.
- Discuss things you can do if you become ill.
- Discuss the importance of having some information handy at all times.
- Decide if you are going to make one booklet covering a lot of subjects or several different booklets covering one area each.

On the Computer:

- Using a publishing program that allows for booklet formatting or a word processor using landscape orientation and 2 columns (leave some space between the columns for the fold), create booklets covering such areas as

  eating properly.

  > food groups

  > regular meals

  exercising.

  > getting enough exercise

  > exercising the whole body

  > exercising safely

  > making exercise fun

  avoiding disease.

  > getting immunizations (You may want to include a chart about when each is due.)

  > practicing cleanliness

  > covering your mouth when you sneeze or cough

  > staying away from people when you have an infectious illness

  > avoiding excessive exposure to the sun

YOUR BODY'S HEALTH NEEDS

avoiding substance abuse.

> not smoking

> not drinking alcohol

> not using illegal drugs

getting enough sleep.

keeping your teeth and mouth healthy.

> brushing and flossing regularly

> visiting your dentist

> being smart about sugary foods

- Illustrate the booklets with drawings, scanned pictures, or cutout pictures.

- I like to use cardstock for the covers.

Internet Links:

- *http://www.healthyideas.com/children/*
  Visit *Prevention Magazine*'s family health page. (Please preview before you let your students go there. It changes frequently.)

- *http://KidsHealth.org/index2.html*
  This site has something for everyone, babies to adults.

DIGESTION

Students enjoy making bulletin boards. Let's make some interesting and informative ones dealing with the body systems.

Grade Level: three to five

Duration: three class periods—one for research, one for writing reports and cutting out illustrations, and one for assembling

Materials: access to the Internet (optional), magazines, drawing paper, research materials (science books, library books, encyclopedias), a word processor, a graphics program, and a printer

Procedure: Research and write up information about each part of the digestive system and what it does. Using pictures and the essays, portray a time line of the digestive processes on the bulletin board.

Before the Computer:

- Discuss the parts of the digestive system.
- Discuss the function of each of the parts and how they work.

  the mouth

  the esophagus

  the stomach

  the small intestine

  the large intestine

On the Computer:

- Using the Internet and other resources, find information and pictures about each of the parts of the digestive system.
- Using the word processor, print summaries of the information
- Save and print pictures from the Internet, do drawings of the parts, and use a painting program or a publishing program to illustrate the summaries.

Internet Links:

- *http://www.bonus.com*
  From the main page choose "Click! Magazine." Then choose issue 14—"Getting Physical." Click on the brain. Now choose "Our Expanding Gut."

- *http://kauai.cudenver.edu:3010/0/nutrition.dir/whatisdi.html*
  An imaginative treatment of the digestive system overview can be explored here.

CIRCULATION

A big book with information on each of the body systems can be kept on display for everyone to read and learn. This page is on circulation, but the book should include all systems and can be done at the same time as the bulletin boards in the previous activity.

Grade Level: three to five

Duration: about two class periods.

Materials: a word processor or program such as *Student Writing Center*, research materials (library books, text books, encyclopedias, and the Internet), and a ring binder

Procedure: Each student will research and write an article to be placed in the class book.

Before the Computer:

- Discuss the parts of the circulatory system.

- Discuss the function of each part and how it works:
    the heart
    the blood vessels
    arteries and arterioles
    veins and venules
    capillaries
    the blood
    the liver

- Discuss the structure of the heart.

- Discuss heart defects and diseases.

- Assign or have each student or group of students choose a subject to research.

On the Computer:

- Each group will research its subject.

- Using a word processor or *Student Writing Center*, write the articles.

- Illustrations make the book more interesting.

- Print the articles and place them in a ring binder for the class to enjoy.

Extension: You may want to have oral reports from each of your "experts."

Internet Links:

- *http://www.bonus.com*
  On the main screen, click on "Click! Magazine." Then choose issue 14—"Getting Physical." After that, click on the brain and then on "You Gotta Have Heart."

- *http://www.super.net.uk/Education/online/thehumanbody/circind.html*
  This is a great site for all body systems.

YOUR BRAIN AND YOUR SENSE ORGANS

See which of your sense organs you use most in various situations.

Grade Level: three to five

Duration: 30 minutes

Materials: spreadsheet program with charting capabilities or a publishing program

Procedure: Have the students record sensory input for a period of time and then chart or graph the results of their observations.

Before the Computer:

- Discussion topics:

    Inside your body are thousands of nerves that are like tiny telephone wires. They are used to send messages to and from the brain.

    Messages between your brain and the rest of your body travel through your spinal cord.

    Different messages go to different parts of the brain.

    Nerves from your eyes, ears, nose, mouth, and skin carry messages to your brain, and your brain sends messages back.

- For 15 minutes, have the students record everything they notice in their environment. You may use the data sheet provided.

- You may want to have different groups record in different situations—on the playground, in the cafeteria, in the library, etc.

- After the information is gathered, you may want to discuss what types of things the students noticed most and least within each category.

On the Computer:

- Open the spreadsheet program.
- Count the number of things observed in each category.
- Label rows with the words sight, hearing, smell, touch, and taste.
- In the column next to your labels, enter the number of things observed.
- Use the charting feature to produce a chart.

    or

- Count the number of things observed in each category.
- Open your publishing program.
- Draw a bar chart with a bar for each of the senses.
- Print the chart.

YOUR BRAIN AND YOUR SENSE ORGANS *(cont.)*

Internet Links:

- *http://www.weta.org/weta/eod/mos_resource.html*
  Find a list of library books to read about the senses here.

- *http://innerbody.com/htm/body.html*
  This is an interactive human body. If you click on one of the tiny buttons, it will tell you about that body part.

- *http://www.4kids.org/coolspots/brainsweat/*
  "The Science of Brains...A Study of Nerves"—here you will find out cool facts about the brain and nervous system.

- *http://www.exploratorium.edu/exhibits/exhibits.html*
  Fool your senses with some of the activities at the Exploratorium.

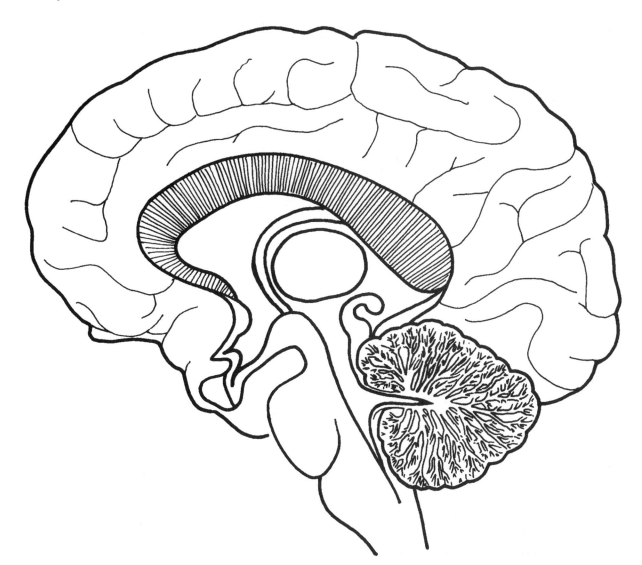

YOUR BRAIN AND YOUR SENSE ORGANS *(cont.)*

Sight	Touch	Smell	Hearing	Taste

MOVEMENT AND GROWTH

Learn the types of joints that help us move our bodies.

Grade Level: three to five

Duration: one class period

Materials: cardstock, a publishing program

Procedure: Create a "What's behind the door?" chart to help learn the types of joints in the body.

Before the Computer:

- Talk about the types of joints in the body and how they work.

    hinge joint

    saddle joint

    ball and socket joint

    plane joint

    fixed joint

- Talk about where each type of joint is located.

On the Computer:

- Using a publishing/drawing program such as *Print Shop* or *Print Artist*, create a template with evenly spaced rectangles.
- On one copy of the template, print the types of joints in each rectangle.
- Print this sheet, using regular paper.
- On another copy of the template, put the names of (or pictures of) the location of the corresponding joint.
- Print this sheet, using cardstock.
- On the top sheet, cut the sides and bottom of each rectangle.
- Glue or staple the edges of both sheets together so that when you lift the flap with the type of joint, you see the location of that type of joint on the body.

MOVEMENT AND GROWTH *(cont.)*

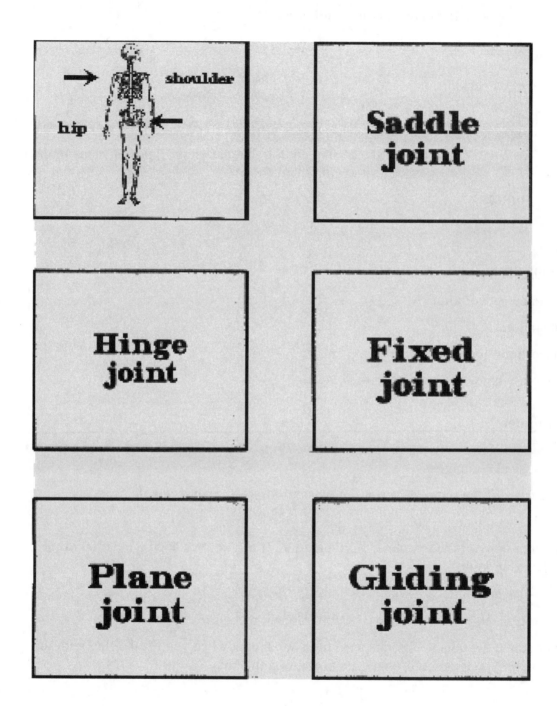

RESPIRATION

Plan and make a slide presentation about respiration.

Grade Level: five

Duration: two class periods

Materials: presentation software such as *HyperStudio* or *Power Point*, access to research materials—library books, textbooks, the Internet, and encyclopedias

Procedure: Make a slide presentation showing the parts and functions of the respiratory system of the human body.

Before the Computer:

- Discuss the parts of the respiratory system.

    trachea

    nasal cavities

    pharynx

    larynx

    lungs

- Discuss the function of each part and how it works.

    Respiration is dependent on both the lungs and the circulatory system working together.

    The lungs absorb oxygen into the blood from the air, and carbon dioxide is expelled into the air from the blood through the act of breathing.

    The circulatory system is required for the exchange of gases between the blood and tissues and for the transportation of gases around the body and to the heart and lungs.

On the Computer:

- Learn to use the presentation program.

- Plan and lay out the cards (slides) that will be included. A planning sheet is provided. (There is another style of planning sheet earlier in the book under "Forms of Energy.")

- This can also be used as a part of a much larger presentation on the systems of the human body.

Internet Links:

- *http://www.purchon.co.uk/science/respire.html*
  This informative article about respiration is text only.

- *http://www.bonus.com*
  Go to "Click! Magazine," then to "Getting Physical," then click on the brain, and finally "A Breath of Air."

RESPIRATION *(cont.)*

Planning Guide

Slide #	**Slide #**
Graphics:	**Graphics:**
Text:	**Text:**
Buttons and Links:	**Buttons and Links:**
Slide #	**Slide #**
Graphics:	**Graphics:**
Text:	**Text:**
Buttons and Links:	**Buttons and Links:**
Slide #	**Slide #**
Graphics:	**Graphics:**
Text:	**Text:**
Buttons and Links:	**Buttons and Links:**

RESOURCES AND
ADDITIONAL REFERENCES

———— . *ABC's of the Human Body.* Reader's Digest Association, 1987.

———— . *Childcraft.* World Book-Childcraft International, Inc., 1990.

———— . *Task Force Clip Art.* New Vision Technologies, Inc., 1995.

Bennett, Steve and Ruth. *The Official Kid Pix Activity Book.* Random House, 1993.

Bryant, Mary Helen. *Integrating Technology into the Curriculum.* Teacher Created Materials, 1996.

Chan, Barbara J. *Kid Pix Around the World—A Multicultural Computer Activity Book.* Addison Wesley, 1993.

Crotts, Deborah. *Earth Science.* Instructional Fair-TS Denison, 1997.

Crotts, Deborah. *Life Science.* Instructional Fair-TS Denison, 1997.

DeBruin, Jerry. *Creative, Hands-On Science Experiences.* Good Apple, Inc., 1980.

Gardner, Paul. *Internet for Teachers and Parents.* Teacher Created Materials, 1996.

Garfield, Gary M. and Suzanne McDonough. *Creating a Technologically Literate Classroom.* Teacher Created Materials, 1995.

Haag, Tom. *Internet for Kids.* Teacher Created Materials, 1996.

Hassard, Jack. *Science Experiences.* Addison-Wesley Publishing Co., 1990.

Hayes, Deborah. *Managing Technology in the Classroom.* Teacher Created Materials, 1995.

Lifter, Marsha. *Writing and Desktop Publishing on the Computer* (Primary). Teacher Created Materials, 1996.

Mackenzie, Joy. *Creative Science Experiences for the Young Child.* Incentive Publications, 1973.

McIntire, Bette. *Plants.* Creative Teaching Press, 1995.

Pereira, Linda. *Computers Don't Byte.* Teacher Created Materials, 1996.

RESOURCES AND
ADDITIONAL REFERENCES *(cont.)*

Rain, Diana, Maria Reidlebach, Rosemary Shmavonian and Karl Schwartz. *Microsoft Office 97.* DDC Publishing, 1997.

Reidl, Joan. *The Integrated Technology Classroom—Building Self-Reliant Learners.* Allyn & Bacon, 1995.

Sharp, Vicki F. *HyperStudio in One Hour.* ISTE, 1994.

Siepak, Karen Lee. *Sound.* Carson-Dellosa Publishing Company, Inc., 1994.

Willing, Kathleen R. and Suzanne Girard. *Learning Together—Computer Integrated Classrooms.* Pemborke Publishers Ltd., 1990.

Wodaski, Ron. *Absolute Beginner's Guide to Multimedia.* Sams Publishing, 1994.

Young, Ruth M. *Hands-On Science.* Teacher Created Materials, 1995.